PEARSON OF CANADA

By JOHN ROBINSON BEAL

SECRET SPEECH: The Failure of Comrade Khrushchev's
Leadership

PEARSON OF CANADA

PEARSON OF CANADA

by

JOHN ROBINSON BEAL

DUELL, SLOAN AND PEARCE
New York

First Edition

Affiliate of
MEREDITH PRESS
Des Moines & New York

Library of Congress Catalogue Card Number: 64-13790

MANUFACTURED IN THE UNITED STATES OF AMERICA FOR MEREDITH PRESS

VAN REES PRESS   •   NEW YORK

To my daughter, Carolyn

Author's Note

CANADIAN AUTHOR Peter C. Newman once noted an aversion in Canada to books about living public figures. He considered it probably unique to his country and ascribed it largely to a lack of literary sophistication. Whatever the reason, in Canadian publishing this aversion has left a gap between the massive, heavily footnoted tome examining several years in the life of a dead prime minister, and the campaign-year paperback compiling what information exists about a would-be statesman.

This book aims between the two extremes, seeking to provide new information about a man who has attained contemporary world importance, to give insight into his motivations, and to examine the pattern of his career. It bears internal evidence of Mr. Pearson's cooperation, but the reader should understand that concept and execution were solely the author's, and it is in no sense an "authorized" biography. For the help provided by the prime minister and his staff within the somewhat stringent limits of their time during the period when the work was in progress, as well as to members of his family, I express my sincere thanks. I am grateful also for the help of numerous individuals who have worked or been in contact with him over the years—members of a circle so wide that time did not permit consulting all who might have contributed.

JOHN ROBINSON BEAL

Contents

Illustrations

PEARSON OF CANADA

1

The Pearson Phenomenon

THE MANNER in which Lester Bowles Pearson became the fourteenth prime minister of Canada was in keeping with the curious air of velleity that had accompanied his steady progress in a long and distinguished career.

Presumably he had been pursuing the job since he became head of the Liberal party in January, 1958, and leader in the House of Commons of Her Majesty's Loyal Opposition. In the five subsequent years it seemed as if he did want to head the Canadian government, but not very much. And on the night of April 8, 1963, when the votes were being counted in the election that elevated him to power, it seemed the voters wanted him to take over from John George Diefenbaker, but not very much. On the electoral applause meter, once the trend was clear enough, the needle trembled between 126 and 128 seats in the House for the Liberals, when 133 was needed for the barest of majorities. Later in the week, when the armed-services vote was added to the civilian tally, the Liberals had won a solid base of 130* seats, 36 more than the Diefenbaker Conservatives. But the magic number 133 still eluded Lester Pearson.

Pearson, of course, professed from the beginning that he wanted to lead his party back to power. This is required of politicians. His campaign statements to this effect never seemed to carry conviction, and one reason was that at the outset his heart did not appear to be behind them. A man capable of objective introspection, Pearson was credited by his intimates with realizing that the Mackenzie King–St. Laurent Liberal regime, under which he had been foreign minister, had developed serious character flaws in the twenty-two years it held continuous power before it went down to defeat in 1957.

Whatever he said in public, Pearson gave the impression of a man handicapped with a sense of fairness that required giving the opposition a chance to show what it could do. Somewhere midway in Diefenbaker's second Parliament the conviction hardened in Pearson that the opposition was bungling the job. Those of his inner circle who knew the fire of determination that glowed within him saw it grow in the light of that conviction; before he finally was elected he wanted very much to be prime minister. Dislike of his adversary's methods and manners provided an additional charge to

* A subsequent recount in the Quebec constituency of Pontiac-Temiscamingue resulted in a tie, resolved by the vote of the returning election official, in favor of the Progressive-Conservative candidate. Although this outcome was then carried into the courts, the immediate effect was to divide the House of Commons between the parties as follows: Liberal, 129; Progressive Conservative, 95; Social Credit, 23; New Democratic, 17; Independent Social Credit, 1. There are a total of 265 seats in the Canadian House.

the fuel of his motivation. Yet something in his make-up still clouded the public's view of Pearson as a politician, and gave rise to the major cliché about him in his opposition years: he lacked decisiveness; he was not a "leader"; he had qualities that might make him an admirable prime minister, but he could never get elected.

"We do not suggest to the voters," said the *Toronto Globe & Mail* in its lead editorial on election day, April 8, 1963, "that in electing a Liberal government they would be electing the greatest government in Canadian history. But we do suggest that Mr. Lester Pearson is a sensible, honest, decisive man who would do his best to live up to that promise."

The comparative faintness of this praise illuminates one surprise of the Pearson phenomenon: that a man possessing Pearson's public image was able to get enough votes to win an election in a democracy.

Attainment of office in the political subdivisions of the North American continent requires one set of talents to win the electorate's approval and an entirely different set, in some cases diametrically opposed, to perform the job once elected. A candidate can win public fancy by displaying a flair for dramatizing himself or for mesmerizing audiences, or by engaging in such ritualistic practices as accepting honorary chieftainships in Indian tribes. None of this applies to his task after election, except as he seeks return to office; indeed, the same *Globe & Mail* editorial was infinitely more bitter about Diefenbaker than it was friendly to Pearson, since by then Diefenbaker was living proof of the disparity between campaigning and governing. "Mr. Diefenbaker has destroyed the Conservative Party," it said. "This great nation is in peril because it has been betrayed by an indolent and indecisive leader who would not lead, by a man who clung, and would still cling, to an office which he does not have the capacity to fill."

Rarely, in fact, are the two sets of qualifications—the talents of the political spellbinder and those of the responsible statesman—combined in one person. They were not combined in Diefenbaker, nor in Pearson. Pearson could never hope to attain the ability for two-way communication with an audience that Diefenbaker possessed to a superb degree. The marvel is that Pearson did make the attempt to superimpose the stump speaker on the diplomat and succeeded well enough.

Equally rare is the spectacle of a man winning high elective office without having put years of driving personal ambition behind it. Competition is always keen for the great plum of being head of government. It is usually the kind that brings out the killer instinct in politicians and requires equal ruthlessness to overcome. From one end of Canada to the other, Diefenbaker audiences were made aware that the ambition to be prime minister had burned bright in him from the time when, as a newsboy in Saskatoon, he sold a paper to the then incumbent, Sir Wilfred Laurier, took his quarter, conversed with him half an hour, and—he told the story with the kind of punch line that delights an audience—finally told Sir Wilfred he had no more time to waste talking but had to get along with his paper deliveries.

Pearson, who also sold newspapers as a boy, embarked originally on an academic career. Each major turning point came without personal direction toward a preconceived ultimate goal. It was not that he drifted before such opportunities as were presented; there were times when he rejected alternative courses or, as during his years of activity with the United Nations, was denied them. But it was not by conscious desire he gave up teaching to enter diplomacy; it was with reluctance he stepped from diplomacy to enter politics as foreign minister under Louis St. Laurent; and when defeat of the Liberal government in 1957 ended that episode, he would have been happy enough to return to teaching and writing had he not been persuaded that no one else could rebuild the crushed structure of the party he believed in. That he, Lester Pearson, the apolitical diplomat and reluctant candidate, actually did reinvigorate a moribund party and restore it to power was the most surprising aspect of the phenomenon.

The way it came about tells a good deal about contemporary Canada.

One of the paradoxes of North America is that so many residents of the United States know so little about their close neighbor, a country they visit more than any other, and the one to which access is easiest of all. Their geographies have impressed them with Canada's size, but not necessarily that it stretches six-and-one-half time zones to the U.S. four. The New Yorker forgets that longitudinally St. John's, Newfoundland, is a third of the way to England, and the San Franciscan that Whitehorse, Yukon Territory, is a third of the distance to Hawaii. On their summer forays north of the border U.S. tourists see the Red Ensign on the flagpoles, but they are not necessarily aware that the flag is only semiofficial. The nation still lacks a distinctive banner of its own because of a violent and purely emotional dispute between Canadians of English and French stock. The traveler takes note of the somewhat different look of French Canada, with its French

7

or bilingual signs, not knowing, perhaps, that here is no counterpart of Cajun Louisiana but a fiercely nationalistic people unreconciled to the fact that their status as equal partners with British Canada has depreciated, in actual practice, during the nearly ninety-seven years of Canadian Confederation. The redcoated Mounties, the black-busbied soldiers changing guard on Ottawa's Parliament Hill, all remind the U.S. vacationer that he is seeing a foreign land; but as he tools across the spacious countryside in his family sedan, he stops at familiar-looking motels, follows standard traffic signs, and gets his accustomed service at the filling stations and stores. It is not surprising he remains ignorant of the fact that Canada is still as loosely organized politically as were the thirteen states prior to adoption of the United States Constitution and that each of the ten provinces retains greater individual autonomy than do any of the fifty states of the Union.

Canadians, on the other hand, know quite a lot about the United States. Eighty per cent of them live within range of U.S. television and radio stations. Their newspapers cover American events in great detail. Merely by reading his own press and watching or listening to national broadcasts, the Canadian knows, for instance, who is maneuvering for the Republican presidential nomination. He is much more likely to be aware of policy disputes among the Pentagon's Joint Chiefs of Staff than of feuding among his own armed services. United States coverage of Canadian events, however, is so skimpy that it takes an event as sensational as the unsuccessful "cabinet revolt" against Diefenbaker in January–February, 1963, to prod American communications media into sending correspondents to find out what's going on.

8

Pearson tells a few stories on himself that illustrate the point. Once, when he was serving at the United Nations and his name was prominent in the news, he was watching a television quiz show in New York. A lady contestant, with several hundred dollars at stake, was asked to name the foreign minister of Canada. "That's an easy one for her," he thought. The contestant obviously didn't know, but she wasn't going to give up the prize without a try; she came up with "Vincent Massey." Massey was then governor general. Certainly no Canadian quiz contestant would have flunked if asked who was the U.S. secretary of state—John Foster Dulles.

Another incident occurred after Pearson's stunning election defeat in 1958. He had gone to spend the Easter vacation with friends in Florida, where he felt he was safely away from all mention of the campaign he had just been through. Turning on the radio to get the news, he heard a commentator describe how the Liberal party under "Liston B. Parsons" had been all but exterminated in Canada. "Well," Pearson remarked to his host, "that's one time I'm glad they got the name wrong."

For the average North American, U.S.-Canadian relations amount to ignorance on the one side and fascination on the other. To the Canadian, American ignorance seems based on complete indifference. The indifference hurts; the ignorance, at least, is always good for a laugh. To the American it comes as a shock to learn that Canada's fascination with his country is at least partly based on worry and resentment. As Pearson himself put it, when he was minister for external affairs, in a California speech explaining his country's desire to maintain a "separate Canadian national personality":

"We are worried about the sheer weight of American pressure, exercised, if you like, quite unconsciously and I know with friendly intent, on this national ideal. Canadianism is, in one sense—perhaps too great a sense—a defensive reaction against the friendly pressure of the United States of America, which, if we did not so react, would engulf us. Frankly, we don't wish to be engulfed."

The American's shock stems from his feeling that he doesn't want to engulf anybody, and why should anyone suspect it? He forgets, if he knew, that as recently as 1911 a speaker of the House of Representatives, Champ Clark, spoke in terms of the Stars and Stripes flying over North America clear to the North Pole. The Canadian remembers, or he is reminded. The American might well ponder a crisp and perhaps unconsciously meaningful remark on the subject made to the House of Commons by Social Credit leader Robert N. Thompson: "The Americans are our best friends, whether we like it or not." Is friendship possible on a "like it or not" basis?

One of the postwar complaints of America's allies has been that the United States pays attention to them only when they cause trouble. Canadians would agree; it seems to them that only after evidence of anti-American sentiment impinged on the American consciousness did the U.S. turn to find out why. Those press emissaries who traveled north to report sent back the word: we can no longer take Canada for granted. True, but scarcely a sufficiently profound conclusion on which to base relations with one's most important trading partner. Suppose the U.S. public suddenly developed a great curiosity about Canada, feeling it was time to study seriously the character of this neighbor. What conclusions would it reach about the Canadian psyche?

We might find some clues to the answer if we looked through the eyes of an emigrant. Let us assume a politically sophisticated American, well acquainted with the U.S. and a sometime tourist in Canada, had moved to the capital, Ottawa, just as the country entered the decade of the sixties, when Lester Pearson was leader of the Opposition. Let us assume he understood reasonably well the organization of the Canadian parliamentary system, but was no less ignorant of its practice than any careful reader of U.S. publications.

Most likely his first impression would have been one of surprise that Canadians were rather sensitive; surprise, for example, that an innocent remark like "you can't tell the difference between Canadians and Americans" was not necessarily accepted as a compliment. Quickly he would have learned about the "search for a Canadian identity" going on among the country's intellectuals.

Canadian sensitivity probably would have struck him as having a curiously feminine tinge to it. Take, for example, Ottawa's private reaction to the appointment of Livingston Merchant as U.S. ambassador. It was his second assignment to the Ottawa embassy, and though the selection was praised editorially, in personal conversation with Americans, some Canadians asked "Why? Why is Washington sending Merchant back?" They seemed to suspect that some slight was intended by the reassignment of a man who had served before, instead of the selection of a new man; when in fact the State Department, only too anxious to please Canada, currycombed its roster to find one sure of favorable acceptance, and picked Merchant because he was known to have been most popular during his first term.

Similar touchiness was displayed when Canada entered into a contract to sell wheat to Communist China. Huge quantities were involved and all available shipping facilities, including tankers, were required. Special blowers were being used to load grain into the tankers, and at one point the U.S. Treasury Department routinely stopped the export of some blowers that had been ordered from the U.S. The shipment was stopped because of a technicality in export regulations, a technicality capable of being reversed—as it was within about twenty-four hours—but Canadians immediately leaped to the conclusion that since the U.S. had an embargo on all trade with Red China it was seeking to prevent Canada from trading there too. Washington's quick action to permit export of the blowers mollified the Canadians. In fact, it seemed to leave them somewhat chagrined over their needless excitment and less suspicious of the U.S., until Diefenbaker sought unsuccessfully to revive the latent suspicion in the 1963 campaign.

Some reactions of our immigrant American would have come as "double take" impressions. It would have taken him some time, for example, to realize that when a nation does not maintain armed forces for a possible instant-death fight with a mortal enemy, its mental attitude toward national preparedness will be different from the attitude to which he is accustomed. This realization would have led to an appreciation of the degree to which the Canadian rebels at being caught willy-nilly between two great antagonists, but surely it would have caused him to wonder how some Canadians could emotionally reject the cold logic that whatever the mission—defensive or offensive—it behooved them to supply their armed forces with the most effective weapons available. In short, the national soul-searching over nuclear weapons would have seemed a shade hysterical to him.

On a more domestic plane, our immigrant would have been puzzled, and quite disillusioned, by the pettiness of Canadian politics. As an observer of Canada from abroad he would have held Canada in high regard as a solid, competent member of the international community. He would have an impression based on the splendid fighting record of Canadians in two world wars and on the country's good reputation in diplomacy, to which Pearson had contributed so largely. To discover that the provinces acted toward the federal government like teen-age brats toward their parents would have left him with a letdown feeling. As a student of the parliamentary system and the theory of "responsible government" he could have understood the strict party discipline that prevails in Parliament, even though it made the back-bench M.P. look like the most underprivileged man in Canada compared to a member of the U.S. Congress; the disillusion would have come with the discovery that, despite the tradition of strong party loyalty, provincial interests invariably transcend party ties. He would have been justified in concluding that the average politician's motto was: "Province above party; region above nation."

Finally, as he sought to grapple with the mystique of "biculturalism," the immigrant would have begun to understand the confused state of the Canadian personality in the decade of the sixties.

The decision of Great Britain's Canadian colonies to join in confederation in 1867 was based, he would have learned, on agreement that the French and English stock would be coequal under safeguards set up to preserve their two cultures, languages, and religions. But an agreement that seemed acceptable in theory almost a century ago had failed by the 1960's to work out equitably in practice, with the French minority numbering only about one-third of the population of 18 million and concentrated chiefly in one province, Quebec. With nine of the provinces under English-speaking dominance and only one under French, our observer could have understood how the French stock felt reduced to second-class status. But its demand for recognition of equal status must have seemed rather artificial in view of the way in which Canada had developed, and would have caused him to wonder whether in fact biculturalism is a viable basis for nationhood. How could there be a "Canadian identity" if part of the country insisted on having a "French identity" and part an "English identity"? What about the refugees from Europe, the "ethnics," or "new Canadians," who made up almost a third of the population? Would it not require assimilation by one side or the other, or a fusing of races as under the U.S. "melting pot" theory, before a country could develop a truly distinct identity? Wasn't it assimilation that made England England after the Norman Conquest? Wasn't it assimilation that kept China China in the face of repeated invasions?

There is a story, possibly apocryphal, that when Franklin D. Roosevelt became President of the United States in the midst of the great depression, an admirer gushed: "You'll be the greatest American President." To which he is supposed to have replied: "Either the greatest or the last." An observer contemplating the problems of Canadian unity when Pearson became prime minister in 1963 might also have applied the mordant thought to him: if he solves the French-English problem in lasting fashion he could go down as the greatest of his country's leaders; if not, he could be the last prime minister of Canada as it has existed since 1867.

2

Bibles and Baseball

LESTER B. PEARSON is a man of average size at 5 feet 9 inches and 173 pounds, with hazel eyes, thinning gray hair that tends to drift down over his forehead when he speaks, and a pleasant Irish face. During his opposition years newspaper cartoonists despaired of his lack of features distinctive enough to caricature and did what they could with his addiction to bow ties, even after he took to wearing four-in-hands. He habitually wears dark suits, chosen for him by Mrs. Pearson. His speaking style is more suited to the lecture platform than the political stump. In the House of Commons, his favorite stance for a major address is to stand with a sheaf of notes in his left hand and his right hand in his trouser pocket. He is more inclined to emphasize sentences with motions of his body and head than with manual gestures, and when he uses his hands to stress a point he tends to use short, chopping motions. With small groups or specialized audiences he conveys an air of sincerity and reasoned intelligence. As a political debater his strongest feature is the Adlai Stevenson type of spontaneous quip.

Pearson was born on April 23, 1897, in Newtonbrook, Ontario, a village long since swallowed up by the growth of metropolitan Toronto. He was the second of three boys in the family of the Rev. Edwin Arthur Pearson, a Methodist minister, and Annie Sarah Bowles. The stock was Irish on both sides. Their eldest son, Marmaduke, known as Duke, became an executive of a leather-company subsidiary of Armour & Co.; now retired, he lives near Boston. The youngest son, Vaughan, who never married, runs a small investment brokerage business in Toronto.

There is an interesting parallel in the early upbringing of Pearson and that of another figure who made his mark in diplomacy, John Foster Dulles. Not many years previously and not very far away, Dulles was brought up as the son of a Presbyterian minister. In both cases the influence of a religious family impressed itself early in the process of character formation. Those who detected a "Presbyterian conscience" in the Dulles foreign-policy motivations will have no difficulty noting a "Methodist conscience" in Pearson's. Although Dulles was raised at Watertown and Auburn, New York, at the other end of the same Great Lake as Pearson, the fact that an international border passed between them did mean that they absorbed different traditions and as youths studied different national histories. But the pioneer background of the two families was quite similar.

They were similar, too, in that the maternal side of the family exerted the greater influence. In the case of Dulles it was the Fosters whose pioneer days he remembered. In

17

Pearson's case, what records existed of his paternal ancestors were lost when a family Bible was destroyed by fire. His grandfather, the Rev. Marmaduke Pearson, was a Methodist minister who filled various pulpits in the Toronto area. He had been born in Dublin where his father, also named Marmaduke, had married a Kate Pritchard and with their family of three boys moved in 1847 to New York, where an older brother had settled. But after two years in New York, Lester's great-grandfather transferred to Toronto as representative of a linen agency, and there the family grew until it included seven boys. The elder Marmaduke once lived on John Street and operated a store on his own property, on the southwest corner of Richmond and Yonge Streets, a location worth millions today.

Lester's minister-father and minister-grandfather, Edwin and Marmaduke, were both Conservatives, while his mother's family were all Liberals. Pearson's mother, who died in 1962, once remarked to an interviewer: "My, what a Tory Lester's Grandfather Pearson was! I don't know what made Lester a Liberal. His father was a Conservative, too. He said he voted for the best man, but the best man always turned out to be a Conservative." The father died in 1934, victim of a ruptured appendix improperly diagnosed because he had never been ill before. Both Pearson's father and grandfather were enthusiastic baseball fans and players and instilled in Lester a lifelong interest in the sport. When his grandfather was old and nearly blind Lester took him to a game in Toronto and described it to him, play by play. Pearson's mother said that as a boy Lester worshiped his father despite his discipline, which involved an occasional spanking; for at

18

other times his father was always ready to play ball with the boys or go ice skating.

Pearson knows more about the Bowles side of the family than about the Pearsons. In 1951, when he was eighty-seven, a maternal uncle, Richard P. Bowles, who was chancellor of Victoria College of the University of Toronto when Lester studied there, set down a family history. It included information Lester's uncle had gotten from his own grandmother, Nancy Bowles, Pearson's great-grandmother.

From this account it appears that the clan traces back to an Englishman named Bowles who was sent to Ireland as a member of Oliver Cromwell's army of subjugation and married an Irish girl. A descendant named Charles Bowles, who lived at Tipperary, married a Nancy Barrie in 1824 and set sail from Wexford for Canada some time thereafter. They landed six weeks later at Quebec and by stagecoach, lumber wagon, and St. Lawrence River boat made their way up Lake Ontario to York, the village that grew into Toronto but which at that time was noted chiefly for its mud.

Charles worked for two years as a stonemason, laying cellar walls and building chimneys for the log houses being erected as immigrants began flowing into Canada as a result of the end of the Napoleonic Wars in Europe. But he had been lured to the New World by the prospect of homestead land. One day a stranger sold him a deed for one hundred acres, supposedly including a log house, for $120. Charles and Nancy acquired a yoke of oxen and an ox sled, and loading it with all their belongings, set out to the northwest for their new home.

They spent the first night at Tullamore, but on the second day the road degenerated into a mere trail through the woods.

The going was laborious over fallen logs, down gullies, and through small streams. As dusk approached they feared they were lost and prepared to spend a night in the woods; but when it became dark, they noticed a light. It proved to be the cabin of Adam Glazier, a homesteader near their own plot of land, who with pioneer hospitality put them up for the night.

Charles was amazed to learn from Glazier there was no dwelling on his land, but was reassured when Glazier said all the neighbors within reach would bring their axes and help him put up a shanty. According to Nancy's account to her grandson, a roof was made of poles covered with long strips of hemlock bark. This was later replaced with basswood logs, split and troughed out, and laid in interlocking U's to carry off the rain. The shanty served them until they could build a more substantial log cabin with a big fireplace. Nancy's stories of how Charles once went out to "chase a hog out of the grain" and flushed a black bear, of the wolves that lurked nearby, of the deer they saw, of the johnnycake and maple syrup they lived on, and of how she carried harrow pins from the blacksmith shop five miles away, made a vivid impression on her grandson.

When the Crimean War sent the price of wheat soaring to $2.50 a bushel, the Bowles family prospered sufficiently to build a brick house, erected on a cash outlay of $150. Charles made the bricks and paid a carpenter-bricklayer twenty cents a day and board to help him. Pine boards were available for the cost of getting his own trees sawed.

The pioneers of the North American continent were deeply religious, and Charles Bowles was no exception. Before any church was established in the settlement he used to walk five miles every Sunday morning to a Methodist "class meeting" at Campbell's Cross. "In my boyhood," notes the family historian, "when the second generation had arrived and the forest had been pushed back to a little strip of woodland at the rear of the farms, and turnpiked roads had been opened and communications everywhere established—even then such was the religious impact from those pioneer days that I can recall only one member of the community who did not regularly present himself in the House of God."

Charles and Nancy Bowles had one daughter and three sons: Eliza, John, Thomas—who was Lester Pearson's grandfather—and George. The children all got a backwoods education. "In those days," runs the family chronicle, "anyone could authorize himself to teach, rent a building in any community, and take in any who would pay the fee he asked."

All the Bowles boys became farmers, and all displayed a flair for public speaking. All three were local preachers, a species of Methodist minister now virtually extinct but then outnumbering the ordained ministry nearly ten to one. Any member of the church with a fervent spirit could, after some instruction in doctrine, be licensed to preach, and Richard Bowles remembered the minister who licensed his father: "Brother George, I have examined all the theologies of all the churches and I must say I find some little taint of error in all of them except the Methodists'." He also recalled a quarterly conference at which the presiding officer announced: "There will be services tonight at all the appointments. Brother John Bowles will preach at Macville, Brother Thomas Bowles will preach at Sandhill, and Brother George Bowles will preach at Mono Road."

The family historian records that although all three

brothers were dependent on their farms for support of their families, their interests were elsewhere.

"I heard them many times in conversation and I cannot recall ever hearing them discussing how to feed hogs or fatten cattle or fertilize soils," he wrote. "Never did I hear them debating the feed value of different kinds of fodder. The preacher, and his last Sunday's sermon, was a frequent topic. I have heard them in hot argument as to whether Adam Clark's commentary on the Bible or Benson's was the better, my father sticking up for Benson, the volumes of which he had perused from Genesis to Revelations.

"So too they loved to give their views on the characters of great men, living and dead. Once I listened to a heated argument as to whether Oliver Cromwell was or was not a Christian. My father contended that he was. This was too much for Uncle John, who had read Carlyle's *Life and Letters of Cromwell,* and whose mind was filled with pictures of the awful cruelties inflicted on the Irish. I have heard them all agreeing that the Presbyterian doctrine of the perseverance of the saints was not only false to Scripture but a most highly dangerous doctrine.

"Often they talked politics, but as the three of them were 'Grits' * there was little debate or controversy. And indeed their discussions went more to personalities than to political measures. They were Irish, and Irish interest invariably set-

* The Reformers of early Canada were nicknamed "Grits" after one of their leaders had called in a speech for men of "clear grit" to join the reform movement. The term is now applied to the Liberals, who succeeded the Reformers. Donald Creighton's standard history of Canada, *Dominion of the North,* notes that "The Grits, who were the true heirs of the Mackenzie tradition, drew much of their strength from the agrarian frontier."

tled on persons rather than measures or things. So it was as a boy I heard much of such men as John Hilliard Cameron, Oliver Mowat, George Brown, John A. Macdonald, Alex Mackenzie, Richard Cartwright, Charles Tupper, Edward Blake, and others. I well remember the contrast they used to make of Mackenzie and Macdonald. Over against the smooth ways and friendly suavity of Sir John they would set the stern honesty and uprightness of Alexander Mackenzie.

"But while the discussions of these three brothers ranged far and wide in history and politics, national and parochial, their minds gravitated always to religion and church affairs."

Lester's grandfather, Thomas, gradually branched out into activities other than farming. His brothers felt he was too worldly—he played checkers. He drew up real estate contracts, deeds, and wills, valued properties for mortgage companies, and served as executor of estates. He entered public life; for fifteen years he was reeve of Chungacousy township, and served as warden of Peel County. Three times he ran for Parliament from Peel, but each time unsuccessfully. He had four sons and three daughters. Annie, Lester's mother, was the youngest daughter.

This was the background Pearson inherited as a boy in turn-of-the-century Toronto. It was similar on both sides of the family, but Pearson thinks the Bowles influence was dominant. "That clan of Irish Methodists was very jolly and very Irish but very strict and puritan at the same time," he says. "I think they had a lot to do with the atmosphere of the home in which I lived, because my mother brought a lot of that with her. But so did my father."

The Pearsons knew the genteel but extreme poverty of life on a minister's salary. In the communities clustered around

Toronto at the time the Rev. Edwin Pearson was preaching the average pay of a Methodist minister was around seven hundred dollars a year. The parson moved often because his church believed in the system of switching "charges" every three or four years.

"We had to be on our best behavior," Vaughan Pearson recalls of the boys' childhood. "You know how it is with minister's families." But puritanical rules had relaxed considerably since the days when Grandfather Tom raised eyebrows by playing checkers. "There was nothing narrow-minded about my family," says Vaughan.

Lester received good grades in school, but he was far from a bookish lad. His father was a keen sports fan and taught all three sons baseball, hockey, and football. Both Lester and Vaughan played semi-pro baseball at one time. Lester played for one summer with the Guelph Maple Leafs. One of his old teammates got into a dispute with him over which position he played—for memories tend to fade—denying that Lester had played third base. "He didn't have the arm to throw from third," the teammate claimed. "He was a good glove man, but not much of a batter." Pearson's enthusiasm for all sports stayed with him through his entire scholastic career. Even as prime minister he can be distracted from official duties by a baseball game on television.

Canadian confederation was just one generation old at the time of Pearson's birth. French-speaking Quebec, or "Lower Canada," and English-speaking Ontario, or "Upper Canada," had made a previous attempt at political coexistence in 1840 and in the process had achieved the principle of responsible, autonomous government, a significant early step in the evolutionary process of gaining independence from Great Britain.

But quarrels between the French Catholics of the East and the English Protestants of the West threatened to fragment Canada again into pockets of separate British colonies, until Sir John A. Macdonald and a like-minded group of nation-builders put across the concept of wider union. Only Ontario, Quebec, New Brunswick, and Nova Scotia joined the Confederation at first, but it did create an autonomous British Dominion whose unique feature was the guarantee of equal status to the two races involved.

Yet, after a generation, the practice of confederation had done little to blend the two races, insuring only that they preserved their own identities in their own localities. In the Ontario communities of Willowdale, Davisville, Aurora, Hamilton, and Peterborough, where Lester got his elementary and high school education, there was virtually no sign of the duality of Canadianism. Pearson grew up a Toronto-oriented and English-speaking Canadian. Only when he got to Oxford did he study French, and though he had occasion to use French a good deal in the practice of diplomacy he never became really fluent in speaking it. He did make speeches in French in Quebec during political campaigns, but he found them a strain. To this day Canada has not produced a fluently bilingual prime minister except from the French members of the partnership.

Pearson remembers two of his schoolteachers as men to whom he owes a great deal. One was R. F. Downey, who taught "everything" in a small school Pearson attended when he was ten years old. "He was a genius as a teacher," Pearson recalls. "He had a way with boys, and he got me interested in work and trying to do well. He got me to see that while it was important to play baseball and make the baseball team, it was important to win a scholarship too, just as much fun as any other competition." Downey helped him with a public school scholarship in Peterborough. Scholarships were important in the Pearson family. As Vaughan recalls, "I often wondered how my father managed to put three boys through college on a minister's salary, but somehow he did. One thing about being a minister's child—you're bound to get a good education."

Pearson's other teaching influence came from Mike McGarvin, who taught him history at Hamilton Collegiate, just before he went to college. "He got me interested in history particularly," Pearson says. "I've never forgotten those two men."

Lester was ready for college in 1913, at the age of sixteen. He entered the Methodist Victoria College of the University of Toronto and was assigned to a residence hall of which Vincent Massey, later Canada's first native governor general, was dean. Their paths were to cross many times in Pearson's subsequent career.

Pearson's college years were, by his own description, "very disjointed." They were interrupted by three years of war. He was entering his second year at the university in the September following the outbreak of the conflict in 1914. A cadet company was formed at the university under Massey's captaincy, and Pearson enlisted. He was drummer in the company band, and remembers taking part in one sham battle in what is now Toronto's residential community of Don Mills but then was out in the country. He drew the job of running dispatches for the company commander.

Massey had just come back from Oxford, and Pearson remembers him as "very Oxonian at that time, very English, very concerned with trying to make this Canadian college as much like Oxford as possible. He tried to make us wear gowns at meals in the great hall. That didn't go over at all. We preferred to wear sweaters."

Because of his age, Pearson could not get his parents' permission to enlist for combat duty, but he did get leave to put in for service in the medical corps, which he joined in March, 1915. He was permitted to take his exams before he left, and passed, thus completing his second year. He did well in his exams and led his honors-history course for two years. The practice at the time was to grant a full year's credit for overseas service. "I got my third year handed to me." When he came back toward the end of 1918 he entered his fourth year and was able to graduate with a B.A. degree in 1919. "It wasn't much of a university career," he says. "It wasn't until I went to Oxford that I really settled down to get an education."

One day in 1963, after he became prime minister, he was driving past the Victoria College library in Toronto on his way to a civic reception in his honor, and the sight of the building prompted him to tell this anecdote about his enlistment:

"I was in the library in 1915, studying a Latin poet, and all of a sudden I thought: 'War can't be this bad.' So I walked out and enlisted."

Pearson was sent overseas on May 15, 1915, with the Toronto General–University of Toronto Base Hospital; first to England; then to Alexandria, Egypt; and finally to Salonika, in Greece. A classmate who shipped with him recalls: "As privates in the medical corps we pictured ourselves as stretcher-bearers doing deeds of heroism under enemy fire.

We didn't realize when we volunteered that instead of that we would wash floors, clean people's backsides, and empty bedpans."

The unit lived in tents for a year, but later was housed in wooden cottages at a camp within sight of Mount Olympus. Pearson promoted himself a job in the quartermaster's store, but he grew restive in Salonika after a year. The work was hard, but not exciting. One after another of his friends were getting themselves transferred into units destined for combat, and there was a demand in the army for college men to train as officers.

One day Pearson, while on leave in Salonika, learned that his older brother, Duke, had been wounded, and his younger brother, Vaughan, had just arrived in England as an artillery-man. Anxious to see more action himself, he cabled his father, asking him to use his influence with his friend, General Sam Hughes, to arrange a transfer to the infantry, where he hoped to get into combat. Hughes, then minister of militia, was an impulsive man, and he responded by sending a per-emptory cable to the British commander at Salonika: "Send Private Lester Pearson back to England."

This got Pearson sprung immediately from his medical-quartermaster duties, and though he expected to remain a private in the infantry he was given a lieutenant's commis-sion when he arrived in England. Subsequently he transferred to the Royal Flying Corps, which was under tremendous pres-sure to produce pilots. Such was the haste to create what was then a new branch of warfare that Pearson's entire preflight training, including navigation, was compressed into six weeks.

His flight instruction lasted only an hour and a half before he was asked to solo. He took the plane—a Grahame White "box kite"—up and when he came down for a landing saw a wire in his path. Attempting to lift over it, he stalled the plane and crashed. No bones were broken, but he was badly bruised and spent a week in the hospital. Then, as he was going back to Hendon airdrome from London in a black-out during an air raid he stepped off a bus and was hit by another bus that was driving without lights. As a result of the two accidents he was invalided home, spending the remainder of the war as a flight instructor at a field near Toronto.

It was when he transferred to the Royal Flying Corps that he picked up the nickname "Mike," which clung to him for the rest of his life. Friends who went to school with him continued to call him Lester, but those who first met him after the war called him Mike. When he presented himself for flying instruction a senior corps officer remarked: "Lester —that's not a very belligerent name for a man who wants to be a fighter pilot. We'll call you Mike."

Pearson didn't like his partisans to exaggerate his war service. In 1962 he was making a campaign speech in eastern Ontario and the local candidate, in his introduction, made rather flowery references to his "distinguished" war record. Pearson refused to accept such praise. "My war service was just about as undistinguished as it could be," he told his audience. "I managed to stay alive." Then, to soften the rebuke to the candidate, he went on, "One medal I should have got, not in war but in peace—" he interrupted the sentence with a chuckle "—I think I should have got the purple heart in 1958." This, of course, referred to his disastrous defeat in his first campaign as Liberal party leader.

Pearson sums up his war service by saying: "I got hurt

29

before I got a chance to get killed—that's about what it amounts to. Looking back now, there seems to be something that was protecting me. I didn't realize it. I never expected to come back from that war. You got to a point after a few years overseas where you just went on until you were killed, like all your friends were being killed. The only thing that would save you from being killed was being wounded, and getting out of it.

"I did everything I was asked to do. I didn't run away from anything, but as it happened it was very drab, and very unpleasant at times. I longed for some kind of action rather than the kind of life I was leading in the Balkans, where we were practically an entrenched camp. The army had been driven back on Salonika and there was no fighting. We were just holding the city. Soldiers were dying all the time of disease, but I never had a day's illness, not one—never missed one day's duty all the time I was out there.

"Then I joined the infantry at a time when the infantry was having a very rough time, early in 1917. I got a commission, but instead of going off to France as a platoon officer, where my life would have been pretty hazardous, they asked for volunteers for the Royal Flying Corps, where the casualty rate was so high they were begging people to transfer. I thought, why not?"

There was one experience after his return from Salonika that gave him a glimpse of Oxford. He joined an infantry cadet battalion that was training at Wadham College. The poet Robert Graves was his Captain. The contrast between two unpleasant years in the Balkans and the unfolding of English spring in Oxford was a tremendous delight to him.

He recalls, "As a boy I used to read Boy's Own Annual and

Chums, an English magazine which had stories of Oxford college life that were pretty romantic and attractive. It became a kind of dream; if I could only get over to Oxford, and experience that kind of life, living at a college, taking part in the games, and having a tutor and sitting around the fireplace! I never thought I would be able to do it, because it cost a lot of money. But after that spring at Wadham College I thought, if I ever get out of this war alive, somehow I'm going to come back here as an undergraduate."

The chance did come, but not immediately.

3

A Job That Stinks

RETURNING FROM the war for his final year
at the University of Toronto, Mike Pearson played hockey
and football and—foretasting an ability on which he had to
draw heavily in his subsequent career—won an oratorical
contest. His speaking topic was the overthrow of Germany,
and he approached the ordeal quaking because his opponent
was a minister with several years of pulpit experience.

In later years his work required him to speak in public to
innumerable audiences, ranging from the statesmen assembled in the General Assembly at the United Nations to voters
clustered around a back-yard barbecue in his home constituency of Algoma East. Although he never developed the flair
with mass audiences usually associated with political orators,
he learned to express himself logically, often with a quotable
or witty turn of phrase, and proved himself effective with
small groups or specialized audiences.

His first job after college was to find gainful employment. He had thought originally of taking up the study of law at Toronto's Osgoode Hall, but decided against it. The problem, common to many university graduates, of finding one's place in the workaday world, was particularly acute for those who had been through the excitement of war and felt rather at loose ends. Mike remembered that while he was overseas he had received a letter from an uncle, Edson White, who was an executive of Armour & Co. in Chicago and later became its president. At a time when the United States was still neutral, White had written both Mike and his elder brother, Duke, applauding their willingness to serve their country and telling them he would see to it they had jobs in the meatpacking business when they got back.

Mike decided to take him up on the offer, and so did Duke. Both young men had romantic ideas of Chicago as a place where fortunes were to be made by enterprising, hard-working people. Mike had no clear idea of just what kind of job he would get, but in a vague way he assumed it would be something in which he could look forward to going onward and upward and ending as a millionaire.

The response to his request brought him down to earth. It was an order to report for work at 7 A.M. the following Monday at Armour & Co.'s Canadian subsidiary in nearby Hamilton, Ontario. Crestfallen but determined, he reported on schedule and learned what his job was to be: operating a press that shot meat into sausage casings. He also learned that when he did not shut off the tap in time the results were quite messy.

Although Duke stayed with the company, Mike only stuck to the job for about a year. (The fact that he once worked

33

for Armour & Co. prompted the Russians to charge, after he had become internationally famous, that he had once worked for an "armaments company.")

Then Mike was called to Chicago—as a junior clerk in the fertilizer division. He found Chicago a stimulating city and the people friendly, but he was hardly as pleased about his job. While he was there the University of Toronto hockey team on which he had once played came through Chicago on the way home from winning the Allen Cup in Winnipeg, where they had been coached by Mike's old friend and wartime buddy at Salonika, W. A. Dafoe. With typical self-humor, Mike told them how he had fought his way up from sausage stuffer to junior clerk by sheer brilliance, industry, and intelligence. But before the visit was over he confessed: "I've got a job that stinks."

He hesitated to tell his uncle that the meat-packing industry had lost its appeal as a career, lest he seem ungrateful for the opportunity that had been given him. He first sounded out his aunt, expressing his doubts about how her husband would look on his willingness to pass up a business opportunity under the most advantageous kind of sponsorship. She advised him to talk frankly to White.

One day he told his uncle he wanted his advice, and the two went for a walk. With some hesitation Pearson said he did not feel cut out for the meat-packing business; what he really wanted to do was go to Oxford to get some more education and then return to Canada, either as a teacher or as a civil servant. Oxford, it was true, seemed out of reach because it cost money, and he had none; but in any event, he wanted to return to Canada.

To his great relief his uncle promptly approved his ambition. "Go right ahead," he told Mike. "Don't worry about any business prospects you feel you may have lost. Try to find the kind of work you enjoy doing. Not too many people are able to get that satisfaction. Find out what you want to do and stick to it. You may be surprised at where it will lead you."

Pearson rated this advice as among the most important he ever got. He applied for a Vincent Massey scholarship to Oxford, and because his grades were good, he got it. Thus he achieved the seemingly impossible dream inspired by reading the *Boys' Own Annual.*

At Oxford Mike resumed the study of history. Quite a number of Canadians who later achieved distinction in their homeland were studying there at the time, as well as Rhodes scholars from the United States.

Pearson's arrival in 1920 coincided with the postwar revival of sports at the institution. Like most Canadians he was avid about hockey, and he had learned lacrosse as a boy in Canada. He tried out for the varsity teams in both games and won his blues in each. He played lacrosse three seasons, during which he took part in two trans-Atlantic tours of the team to the United States and Canada and was picked for the team that played for the south of England against the north in Britain's annual championship game.

His skill on the ice won him membership on Britain's 1922 Olympic hockey team. His Oxford team, in a Christmas, 1921, holiday tour of Europe, defeated six teams to pile up a score of 87 against 2 for its opponents. At Murren, Switzerland, the Oxford team defeated a Cambridge team 27 to o. *Isis,* an Oxford University publication, commented: "That surely must be a world's record."

As is true of many other traditional school rivalries at Oxford, a good season's record is not as important as beating Cambridge. One year Pearson was on the team that beat Cambridge in lacrosse. Returning home by bus, the team decided that the victory called for a celebration, and there were numerous stops at pubs along the way. Mike himself did not drink or smoke, but the result was that Pearson and a teammate arrived at their lodgings after the closing hour of midnight and had to rouse the porter to let them in.

At 9 A.M. next day the two students received a summons to the office of the dean. Mike bounded up the steps two at a time, muttering: "He can't do anything to us. We just beat Cambridge." His defiant mood quickly dissipated, however, in the actual presence of the dean, a man of forbidding Victorian countenance, with a long beard. The dean conducted the interview on his own terms.

"Is it true," he inquired, "that you gentlemen had to seek admission to the college after midnight?"

Solemnly they admitted it was true.

"Is it true you had no leave to enter after midnight?"

Again they confessed their crime.

"And are you aware that the porter had influenza, and the assistant porter had influenza, and that it was extremely inconvenient?" Without awaiting their reply, he continued: "That will be five pounds for each of you. Good morning, gentlemen."

Without a word, and without mentioning lacrosse or Cambridge, the two miscreants went to the bursar's office and paid their fines. "He would have let us off if it had been cricket," Mike grumbled.

Pearson still counts his two years at Oxford as the happiest in his life. Reminiscing about it he has said, "It was wonderful. I played on all the teams in my college and I loved the subject I was studying, modern history. My tutor, W. C. Costin, became my friend. I had wonderful vacations, playing hockey on the continent with the Oxford team." He also managed to sandwich in a summer at the University of Heidelberg.

Oxford was followed by his appointment in the fall of 1923 as a lecturer in history at the University of Toronto. Among his students was a girl named Maryon Moody, daughter of a Winnipeg physician, who was very popular on the campus and dated a number of students. One of them who corresponded with her after he left Toronto recalls a letter in which she reported: "We've got a very interesting young history professor named Mike Pearson." Some time later she wrote her friend that she and Mike Pearson were engaged to be married.

The marriage took place in Winnipeg on August 22, 1925. It was the beginning of a very happy and rewarding family life and contributed to his subsequent success. Pearson was then earning $1,800 a year. They lived in a small flat in Toronto, shopped together at the market, and Maryon cooked and ran the typical menage of young newlyweds. From the start she took over the running of the Pearson establishment. She managed the budget, paid the household bills, and bought whatever was needed for the family; she even chose his suits and bought the family cars. In his career he found it a great relief to leave the domestic worries to her.

On any college faculty there are always a few members who stand out among the rest in popularity with students, and according to a fellow professor, Pearson was one of these.

His friendly personality made him attractive as a lecturer, and he was soon advanced to assistant professor.

He began to think about getting a doctorate, since higher degrees were a touchstone to academic advancement. The head of the history department, G. M. Wrong, suggested that a history of Canada's United Empire Loyalists might make a good subject for a thesis. Wrong felt that no one had yet written a really good historical study of the group of North Americans who elected to stay under the rule of the British Crown at the time of the American Revolution. "They have become romanticized as great patriots who fled to Canada for king and country," Wrong told him, "but you may find a different story for some of them."

Acting on this suggestion, Pearson and his bride went to Ottawa and went through the archives looking for material on the Empire Loyalists, searching through dusty tomes and examining old letters. During that summer of 1926 Pearson met Dr. O. D. Skelton, who had left Queen's University to organize the newly created Department of External Affairs.

The Pearsons' first child, a son, Geoffrey, was born the following year, and Mike became involved in school athletics as a coach. He was named head coach of hockey and assistant coach of football. Though he found both teaching and coaching very enjoyable, the combination kept him too busy to follow through on his research for a doctorate. When Skelton got in touch with him to ask if he would be interested in taking the examination for first secretary in the diplomatic service, soon to be held at various centers around the country, Pearson felt that he was doing exactly what he had always wanted to do and wouldn't think of leaving. But Skelton had said, "You don't need to accept appointment even if you pass the examination," and Mike agreed to take a shot at it. Only two others from Toronto presented themselves for the test, which was held at the University of Toronto, although about sixty others tried out in other centers. Mike spent three days with Kenneth P. Kirkwood and Hugh Keenleyside writing papers.

Then he went back to his regular duties. In the January, 1927, issue of a college publication, *Acta Victoriana,* he wrote in typical Pearson literary style an article plugging amateur sports as against professional. Under the title of "The Game's the Thing" he wrote:

"It isn't. The 'gate's the thing." No longer is a game possible without a 'gate,' and that cannot be secured without publicity. The result is that before any important sporting event today there is as much ballyhooing as was used in the Middle Ages to commence a crusade. The Americans excel in this. They have become the greatest ballyhooers in history."

In similar disapproving vein he wrote that "millions who have never heard of the nationalist movement in China, hang on the last sentences of Mr. 'Swede' Risberg. The respectable Judge Landis, who deserted the bench for baseball, and $65,000 a year, makes weighty pronouncements with the gravity of a Caesar Augustus. That august assembly, the United States Senate, threatens to desert the consideration of the world court and the conquest of Nicaragua in order to be free to discuss the affairs of a Tyrus Raymond Cobb."

4

Price Spreads and Tennis with Eden

ONE DAY a telegram addressed to Professor L. B. Pearson arrived at Baldwin House, the history building of the University of Toronto. Pearson had undergone an eye test that morning, and his pupils were still dilated with belladonna. Unable to read the message, he went down to the basement, thinking he could see better in the semidarkness. Finding that didn't help, he looked up the janitor and had him read the telegram. It was from Ottawa, and it was notification that Pearson had passed the examination for first secretary in the Department of External Affairs. In fact Pearson topped the list, though he thought his veteran's preference may have weighted the result in his favor.

It was the first of a series of opportunities that changed the direction of Pearson's career. As we have noted, he took the examination more or less by request, without any real desire to enter the diplomatic service. He did not feel driven by financial pressure to change jobs, and he hesitated to leave a job he so thoroughly enjoyed. Nevertheless he decided on the step that took him out of academic life for good.

In August, 1928, he and Maryon moved to Ottawa with their infant son, Geoffrey, and found a small house on Daly Avenue, in the section known as Sandy Hill, which rented for fifty dollars a month. Ottawa was a town where an automobile was not a necessity, and it was a time when a good cook could be hired for twenty-five dollars a month. Later, when the Pearsons did get a car, it was a secondhand Model A Ford.

The external-affairs department was then very small, with scarcely a dozen officers stationed in Ottawa, and missions in Washington, London, Paris, and Tokyo. It was less than ten years since Canada had begun the transition toward taking over control of her own foreign affairs from Great Britain, a development dating from the 1919 peace conference in Paris following World War I. Previously Britain had represented all the dominions in foreign dealings, but at that conference the dominions at their own insistence were represented not only as parts of the British Empire but in their own right as independent countries. Canada's Sir Robert Borden, then prime minister, was one of the dominion premiers who, after some opposition, won the imperial war cabinet's agreement to the dual representation and its acceptance by the Paris conference itself.

By this anomalous arrangement Canada lost the right to vote other than as part of the British Empire delegation, but won the advantage of signing the treaty twice, as a separate plenipotentiary as well as a representative of the British Empire. This recognition paved the way for Ca-

41

nadian membership in the League of Nations the following year, leading to the significant step in 1927 by which Canada's independent diplomatic status was confirmed when she was elected to the League Council.

It was only in the year previous to Pearson's appointment that Canada had sent its first minister to Washington. The independent status of Canada in Washington had been recognized in 1920 by simultaneous announcement in London and Ottawa that Canada would have a minister plenipotentiary "who will have charge of Canadian affairs and will at all times be the ordinary channel of communication with the United States government in matters of purely Canadian concern, acting upon instruction from, and reporting to, the Canadian government." But typically it took the Canadian government seven years to fill the job. Prime Ministers Meighen and King both claimed it was hard to find the right man for so important a job, though the press periodically sprouted stories that it had been offered to Sir Robert Borden, Sir Lomer Gouin, Sir Clifford Sifton, and many others. Finally, however, King named Vincent Massey; and in February, 1927, Massey presented his credentials to President Coolidge.

In the small department existing in Ottawa in 1928, Skelton's purpose was to enlist "bright young men" who would grow with the department. It was the practice in those days for the prime minister to retain the post of foreign minister as well, so that departmental officers did special jobs for the P.M. on assignments that were outside the diplomatic field. In any case, a departmental officer's work involved all sorts of odd jobs.

Pearson's first assignment was to comb through old treaties

of Great Britain and see how many were applicable to Canada. The purpose was to determine how many Canada should keep in force and how many should be abrogated, now that Canada was an independent country. After a few weeks of this straight research job, he was detached and sent on temporary duty to Washington to assist his former cadet captain, Vincent Massey, in discussions with the United States over the *I'm Alone* case. The *I'm Alone* was a rum runner of Canadian registry that had been sunk by the U.S. Coast Guard during a chase; it had been attempting to smuggle in liquor while prohibition was in effect in the United States. Although Pearson was not a lawyer, there were minor diplomatic chores to perform that made his presence in Washington necessary.

In the fledgling Department of External Affairs, however, there were assignments not connected with diplomacy. There was need to use its "bright young men" for other governmental chores. The great depression had hit Canada by the early thirties, and farm income was greatly affected. Complaints from the prairies inundated the government in Ottawa. There was a feeling on the part of farmers that the activity of Winnipeg grain speculators was adversely affecting the prices they received, causing unnecessary price fluctuations. As one response to the situation the government set up a royal commission under Sir Josiah Stamp to study the effects of trading in grain futures, and Skelton was asked to provide someone from the department to serve as the commission's secretary. He picked Mike Pearson.

The commission held hearings in Winnipeg, Regina, and Calgary, and conferred with U.S. officials in Minneapolis and Chicago, eventually coming up with a seventy-two-page report that noted among its acknowledgments: "Finally, we

43

owe much to the very efficient help given by our secretary, Mr. L. B. Pearson, both during our sittings and subsequently in seeing our report through the press." The report itself answered the question whether dealing in grain futures affected the price received by the farmer with a fairly lengthy explanation of the benefits of a futures market, but it also contained this summary:

"All the foregoing may seem very involved and elaborate to the man in the street who likes a plain 'yes' or 'no' to what seems to him a plain question.

"Unfortunately, however, no short statement on an economic matter is ever strictly and absolutely true, and this very natural desire for a plain answer can only be met by statements which are true generally, but leave room for times and cases where qualification is essential.

"However, in brief, our answer to the question submitted is that in addition to the benefits reflected to the producer in furnishing a system of insurance for the handling of his grain, and in providing an ever-ready and convenient means for marketing the same, futures trading, even with the disadvantages of numerous minor price fluctuations, is of distinct benefit to the producer in the price which he receives."

This was the beginning of a practical economic education for Pearson in the elements involved in Canadian domestic politics. This education Pearson's critics overlooked in the 1960's when they wrote him off as a diplomat who was conceded to be outstanding in international affairs but had no feel for the issues that stirred the Canadian voter.

Of even greater importance was his assignment in 1934 to another royal commission, this one examining the whole spectrum of Canada's depression economy under instructions to look into price spreads between the producer and the ultimate customer. No secretary of such wide-ranging inquiry could have escaped acquiring a fund of information about his country, and it filled in an important element of Pearson's background. In addition it first brought him into contact with Walter Gordon, a Toronto accountant, who became one of his closest personal friends. Gordon was one of the commission's staff. This assignment kept Pearson steadily busy for eighteen months, and was responsible for calling him to the attention of high government officials, including the prime minister, R. B. Bennett.

The price-spreads commission was instructed to investigate "the causes of the large spread between the prices received for commodities by the producer thereof and the price paid by the consumers therefor." Under this charter it examined such things as the effect of mass buying by department and chain-store organizations on the smaller businesses, and labor conditions in such big organizations.

The inquiry produced a 499-page report including a tax memorandum by its chairman, H. H. Stevens, pointing out that big businesses had a competitive advantage over smaller rivals through such features as the consolidated tax return, which enabled them to reduce taxes by offsetting profits from successful units with losses from others. The report proposed seventeen amendments to the Dominion's companies act as well as provisions designed to prevent stock-watering and suggested changes in corporation legislation, labor and wage regulation, retail distribution, consumer protection, and combines (antitrust) law. It was part of Canada's economic self-searching, prompted by the hardships of depression, that roughly paralleled the antimonopoly, patent, and other inquiries going on in the United States.

For Pearson this experience was a valuable broadening of interest on the part of a man who had studied and taught history, as well as an influence on the political outlook of one who until then had had little cause to think deeply about the economic aspects of Canadian life. "It was a magnificent education in domestic economic affairs," he said later on looking back to that period. "If they had wanted to educate somebody for a future job in politics they couldn't have done better than give him that job. We covered the whole front of the domestic economy, and it was a great background in the economics of Canada at a time when we were in the depths of the depression."

His service in Ottawa, however, was not confined to such domestic chores. Till 1935, during the seven years he was based in Ottawa, he made occasional trips abroad with Prime Minister Bennett. The external-affairs department did not pay for wives on such trips, and Mrs. Pearson stayed at home with Geoffrey and their daughter Patricia, who was born in 1929. Mrs. Pearson did, however, make one trip to London with him in the early years, to attend the London naval conference. To save money they often shared breakfast; he would order one breakfast, for which he was entitled to collect expenses, and they would divide it.

Bennett took Pearson with him to a commonwealth conference in London in 1934, and on the ocean voyage the prime minister was at work on a list of names he planned to submit for the king's annual "honours list." Mackenzie King, who served his second term as head of government just prior to Bennett, had abolished the "honours-list" system, but Bennett had restored it and was trying out names of worthy Canadians on Pearson and one of his secretaries.

One night on shipboard after he got the list completed he called Pearson to his cabin and informed him: "I've put you down for an OBE." It was intended as reward for the work Pearson had done on the price-spreads commission.

Pearson was surprised. He knew it would cause comment in the external affairs department and that Skelton didn't believe in decorations for his officers. He wondered if Bennett would settle for a promotion instead of a decoration. With an attempt at jocularity he said, "Mr. Prime Minister, I would settle for twenty-five-dollars more a week. I can't raise a family on an OBE." His pay was then about three hundred dollars a month. His allowances on such trips were only enough to cover the cost of his room at Claridge's, where he had to stay because Bennett did, and did not suffice for his other expenses.

Bennett was very annoyed by Pearson's attitude. He snapped: "If you make me change my list again, now that I have it all completed, not only will you not get an OBE, you will not even get a promotion." But he relented; and taking the hint, he saw to it eventually that Pearson got both the OBE and reclassification in grade that carried higher pay.

Working for Bennett, Pearson learned a lot of odd jobs but nothing very specific. He found Bennett a mercurial character, quick tempered and often given to acting more on impulse than judgment. Despite these traits, Pearson developed a real affection for him and appreciated his kindnesses. Later, during World War II, when Bennett was retired and living outside of London, in Surrey, the former prime minister often invited him down for the weekend, providing for

47

Pearson a welcome relief from the tension under which he lived in London during the frequent German air raids.

Pearson got his first foreign post in 1935, in London. Canada's high commissioner there was, by that time, Vincent Massey, and his number-two man was Colonel George P. Vanier, who later became ambassador to Paris and eventually the first French Canadian governor general of Canada. When Vanier shifted to Paris, Pearson moved up to the deputy's job.

At first his duties were not onerous, and London was a welcome change from Ottawa, where he had been working all hours. He compiled dispatches for Ottawa, helped Canadians get in touch with relatives fighting in Spain during the civil war, and assisted with the job of enabling Europeans to immigrate to Canada; in one case he arranged for the migration of a large number of Sudeten Germans to the Peace River district in Alberta.

One of his routine jobs was distributing sixteen-millimeter films on Canada to British schools. He thought the films were of such poor quality that something ought to be done about it. Having become acquainted with the work of an Australian, John Grierson, who had done an excellent documentary on Newfoundland, Pearson arranged for Grierson to advise the Canadian government on production of more suitable films for showing overseas. This initial step from London led to the creation of Canada's National Film Board, which turns out excellent work and has become an important instrument for projecting the national image at home and abroad.

Still another sideline activity of his job was attending meetings of representatives of the Canadian Wheat Board, which was making efforts to dispose of the surplus crops turned out in the prairie provinces. This gave him an insight into one of Canada's major export problems, one that was still with him when he became prime minister.

During his four years in London before he got home leave in 1939, Pearson's most important diplomatic assignments were in connection with various conferences held in Geneva, including sessions of the League of Nations. He got to know Geneva well and grew to love the town clustered around the lower end of its alpine lake, within reach of some of Europe's most spectacular scenery. He played tennis with Anthony Eden occasionally, when Eden headed the British delegation, and even joined a Swiss hockey club, the Servette, which played out-of-town engagements on weekends. During one conference he was asked if he would play for Switzerland on the national hockey team, but that seemed not quite the suitable thing to do. "Things were very free and easy and informal in those days," he recalled later. It was an age when some of Europe's foremost statesmen strolled casually across the Rhône bridges to have lunch in one of Geneva's famed restaurants; an era to which diplomats looked back nostalgically in the years following the second world war when, in the grim conferences between East and West, each foreign minister moved, even to lunch, with a claque of advisers surrounding him, or formally entertained some other delegation in strict keeping with the demands of protocol.

The young diplomat found it exciting to work in the city where Calvin and Knox had preached, to eat in the brasserie where Lenin had plotted the overthrow of the Tsar, to live at the Hotel de la Paix on the quai overlooking Lac Léman where it empties into the Rhône, to rub elbows with the big-name leaders of Europe between the wars. But nothing quite equaled the thrill of sitting down at a League of Nations conference table for the first time as representative of his country.

This occurred under circumstances that tinged the excitement with personal worry. The League was making an effort to cope with the Ethiopian crisis. The issue was the one on which the League foundered: whether to impose sanctions against Italy. Canada's permanent representative, Dr. W. A. Riddell, had appeared to sponsor a proposal to cut off oil shipments to Italy, and back home cautious Prime Minister Mackenzie King was quick to disavow him. Ottawa made it known publicly that Riddell was expressing his personal views and not those of the Canadian government. This made Riddell's position as Canadian representative untenable, and Pearson was sent to replace him temporarily. Pearson knew that under the circumstances he had to avoid taking any initiative in the councils of the nations. "I hated just to sit there and not have any views about anything," he recalled later.

Nothing is so revealing of the formative years of a diplomat as the diary Pearson kept during the years in London. At various times in his life he attempted to keep a daily record of the events in which he was involved, with his comments. He never managed to keep the journal continuously, because at times he became too busy, but the fragments he preserved are richly larded with comments indicating his reactions.

One entry he started on December 31, 1936—the result of a New Year's resolution—discussed the "inside story" of King Edward VIII's abdication as Pearson had heard it from a friend at Buckingham Palace and from "Downing Street sources." According to the story, the king had not really wanted to succeed to the throne of his father, George V, but was persuaded to do so. He determined to accept only on one condition—that he should be able as soon as possible to regularize his position with Mrs. Wallis Simpson through marriage. He abdicated because this condition was frustrated. "Possibly the lesson of the whole thing," wrote the young Canadian diplomatic observer, "is that in the 16th century the king could be both politically and romantically adventurous; in the 17th and 18th centuries he could only be romantically adventurous; in the 20th century he can be neither politically nor romantically adventurous."

A strong Canadian nationalism showed up early, for in the first week of January, 1937, he wrote: "An item appeared in the weekend press which aroused my ire to the effect that the new King, as a part of the rather too obvious attempt to make him into another King George, has announced his determination to ride in English cars only and to reverse the unfortunate precedent of his brother, who, as King of Canada, had the nerve to purchase a Canadian car." Pearson had let a Buckingham Palace friend know "that action of this kind may strengthen the new King's place in the hearts of his English subjects, but would not tend to make him any more popular in Oshawa (the Canadian Detroit) or in other parts of Canada. It will be a long time before certain people in this country realize that the King is the King of more than one country."

On January 7 he wrote that the high commissioner had asked him to list all dispatches the London office had addressed to Ottawa with inquiries that remained unanswered. "This should produce interesting results," Pearson commented, "as our general impression here is that hardly any of our enquiries are ever answered. When we get the information, then we will confront the External Affairs Department with their sins in the vain hope that it might lead them to repentance."

He displayed a healthy skepticism about newspaper rumors, for after lunch one day with several journalists he recorded: "Apparently the adventures of the Duke of Windsor have whetted the appetite of the English public for more. I was assured that the Duchess of ____ is about to sue the Duke for a divorce, naming a lady who was indiscreet enough to be seen in a fortune teller's with the Duke. The Duke of ____ it seems, is enamoured of Mrs. M. So far no suspicion of immorality has attached to two-year-old Prince Edward. No doubt he will be charged shortly with having seduced his nurse."

Nor was he taken in by diplomatic speeches from high personages. After listening to Anthony Eden speak on contemporary British foreign policy in the House of Commons, Pearson's reaction was: "There was rather too much of: why can't everybody be as high-souled and peace-loving as we are?"

A January entry said: "The High Commissioner read to me yesterday the letter which he just received from the Prime Minister requesting the use of my services during the Coronation and the Imperial Conference as a secretary . . . I am not very much enamoured of this prospect as Mr. Mackenzie King is probably one of the most difficult men in the world to assist in the writing of speeches."

He recorded that a diplomatic colleague, having been in England for six years, naturally had wanted to see the coronation of George VI before he left for a new post, but was

Prime Minister Pearson caught in a thoughtful pose.

Mr. and Mrs. Pearson with six of their eight grandchildren. Left to right: Katherine Pearson, Hilary Pearson, Robin Hannah (on Mrs. Pearson's lap), Anne Pearson (with Mr. Pearson), Barbara Hannah, Paul Hannah.

A 1904 family portrait. Left to right: the Rev. Edwin A. Pearson, Marmaduke, Lester, Vaughan (below Lester), Annie Sarah Bowles Pearson.

Private Lester Pearson with the University of Toronto medical unit after its arrival in England in 1915. Pearson is in the top row, second from right.

Signing the Japanese peace treaty for Canada at San Francisco in 1951.

As an experienced diplomat, Pearson was frequently consulted by UN Secretary-General Dag Hammarskjold.

With John Foster Dulles at the 1954 Canadian–United States economic conference. Center: C.D. Howe, Canadian minister of trade and commerce.

Department of State

Fednews

The Pearsons see the sights of Moscow during Russian visit in 1955.

Dwight E. Dolan

Pearson meets Emile Cardinal Léger in Montreal.

Campaigner meets future voter outside a Toronto supermarket.

Pearson comments for news media on election night, 1962, when he failed to win but saw Diefenbaker cut down to minority status.

Pearson's first trip abroad as prime minister re-established friendly relations with the government of Harold Macmillan.

Pearson with Lord Home, British foreign secretary and later prime minister, at Ottawa meeting of NATO.

NATO

Duncan Cameron, Capital Press

Harold Wilson, British Labour leader, calls on the new Canadian prime minister during his London visit.

Duncan Cameron, Capital Press

Pearson reviews honor guard with the late President Kennedy during a visit at Hyannis Port.

ordered by his government to be in Washington that day. "I thought only Canadian governments did things like that," wrote Pearson.

As a Canadian he was disappointed with the "feebleness" of a London *Times* editorial when Canada and the United Kingdom signed a trade agreement. "It would seem," he wrote, "that they reserve their senior leader-writers for such things as the situation in Danzig or the possibility of a change of government in Bulgaria. One of the office boys could undoubtedly be trusted with a leader on Canadian-United Kingdom trade."

He was not too impressed with a conference about press relations at Buckingham Palace. "We sat around the table in great dignity and after an hour or so had decided on a question which could have been settled over the telephone in two minutes, namely, that a representative of each Dominion's press would be permitted to attend the daily press conference at Buckingham Palace. It was Lord Wigram's idea. He is a charming old gentleman who seemed to think that with such a concession as this, Commonwealth relations would be cemented forever." Of the palace press officer he commented: "I was told his chief function is to irritate each day those journalists who are privileged to appear before him."

On March 3 he noted: "I have been asked by the *Fortnightly Review* to write an article on the significance of the recent decisions of the Privy Council throwing out Mr. Bennett's New Deal legislation. I shall have to do it under a pseudonym, as we civil servants are not supposed to publish our ideas on such controversial questions. On the other hand, we civil servants nearly always need a few extra pounds, which I shall hope to receive although both the editor and

I, when we met to discuss the matter, were much too genteel to bring up the question of money."

He attended a dinner of the Royal Empire Society at which he heard a speech by "an old colonial servant who still feels that there should be no constitutional difference between Basutoland and Canada." Pearson wrote that "he irritated me intensely by some slighting references to Sir Wilfred Laurier, Canadian nationalism . . . and progressive ideas generally. I unfortunately let myself go at the dear old gentleman and spent nearly all my time glorifying in my unrepentant Canadian nationalism."

His amusement at governmental red tape showed in his quoting a message from Ottawa concerning one aspect of preparations for the coronation. The work, he noted, "gets more hectic all the time," and telegrams like the following became a daily routine: "Commissioner RCMP states impossible to arrange earlier shipping date for horses than that indicated. Extraordinary noises of street parades are part of regular training but horses are at present undergoing strenuous training in unusual noises. Commissioner does not expect any difficulty will be experienced with horses." He added that the high commissioner, not to be outdone, had sent a reply: "Personal. Am informed on high authority that the most experienced, even the most blasé horse, although habituated to usual and extraordinary noises, will sometimes collapse with terror at sight of bearskin busbies as worn by Guards. Would suggest this aspect of problem should be drawn to attention of appropriate authorities."

Notified that he was to represent Canada at an international sugar conference, Pearson wrote: "The whaling conference may be meeting at the same time, so I hope I don't get my two briefs mixed. It would be most unfortunate if I went to the sugar conference and picked up the wrong speech and started talking about the necessity for preserving blubber and whale oil." Of the sugar conference itself, held the following month, he wrote: "Of course no one here has any idea whatever as to what the Canadian attitude toward this conference is, or even if there is a Canadian attitude. But I was reluctant to say that, so I chatted amiably for 15 minutes ... of course I kept carefully away from the sugar conference itself because I knew nothing about it; I kept even more carefully away from Canadian policy."

One day he was asked to substitute for a Canadian who was unable to keep a date to speak on a British Broadcasting Company program. Pearson found he enjoyed the experience. "It was the first time I had spoken over the wireless and it was an interesting experience made much more interesting by the fact that they gave me five guineas for it. I could hardly be restrained from volunteering to do it again the next night."

Coronation arrangements continued to take up a great deal of time and he was annoyed by the "honor" of being appointed a "gold stick in waiting," or usher, which required endless rehearsals and renting a fancy costume. "My grouse," he wrote, "is that these rehearsals are a sheer waste of time, that any intelligent person could see what he has to do in two minutes, where we already have spent three hours in standing about, being told about things that don't matter. Secondly, my post in the Abbey, unlike those of my Canadian fellow ushers, is away off in the back behind the choir where I shall see nothing of the coronation itself, but as a compensation have a perfect view of those temporary lavatories which a paternalistic government has so thoughtfully provided for its peers and peeresses. Goodness knows they will need them as they will be in the Abbey about 10 hours and most of them are elderly ladies and gentlemen." He said he did not think this would be "sufficient compensation" for the duties of the office "or the five guineas which it will cost me to rent the fancy suit."

Coronation duties caused a lapse in the diary, but when he resumed it he told of his boredom with long rehearsals for duties "a dozen or so cinema girls" could have performed with a single rehearsal, and the explanations about "special cases," such as Lady A, "who was completely paralyzed and would arrive in a wheel chair, accompanied by doctor and nurse, and would have to be 'gold staffed' to her seat in spite of obvious difficulties and watched carefully thereafter for seven or eight hours in case she died." He confirmed that he had not seen the crowning itself, only the door to the ladies' room.

5

Dinner with Churchill

AS THE second world war approached, the work in London grew more and more absorbing. Pearson kept in close touch with British officials, advised Massey, and wrote analytical reports for the government at home, based on British diplomatic dispatches from all over the European continent.

At first neither Stanley Baldwin nor Neville Chamberlain believed Hitler would become enough of a menace to require the British nation to arm for conflict, and in the early stages Pearson was inclined to take the same view. He thought Hitler's first moves represented a phase of German revulsion against the Versailles Treaty, and the effects of economic depression. But when Hitler began his persecution of the Jews and marched into Austria, Pearson became convinced he would stop at nothing, even war, to achieve his goals. Canada, he felt, should reckon on the inevitability of war in

Europe and not allow itself to be hoodwinked by Hitler's claim after each new move that he was making his "last territorial demand." Pearson's cables to Ottawa reflected these views.

One of the incidents that made a deep impression on him and helped him reach this judgment was a small dinner he attended with Winston Churchill in 1938. Churchill at that time was in eclipse, at the lowest point of his prewar fortunes and without a following. He was, however, beginning to build up a school of thought that questioned the policy of the British government. Pearson was invited to a dinner given by a London eating club at which Churchill was the guest of honor.

Churchill spoke gloomily about the situation in Europe, and after the dinner a few of the guests adjourned to a small room to talk further with him. Among the small group that gathered privately—some eight or ten of the twenty who had attended the dinner, someone asked: "Do you really think there is going to be a war?"

"Before I deal with that question," said Churchill, "I would like a Scotch." And, though he had just had an enormous, epicurean meal, he added: "You'd better have them bring a cold beef sandwich with the Scotch." With his superb sense of dramatic suspense and timing, he finished off the sandwich and the drink before he addressed himself to the question.

He had a small table in front of him. Jotting down figures on a piece of paper, he said. "War will break out in about a year." His figures listed the strength of Nazi Germany in fighting planes and army divisions; they were figures he had used in public speeches, which England was inclined to discount as exaggerated. "These are correct figures," he insisted. Against them he listed the strength of France, commenting that the French military system was rotten and its forces were shoddily equipped; and he listed the relatively weak forces Britain had to withstand an assault. "It will only take the Nazis a few months to break through," Churchill predicted to his fascinated listeners.

Churchill's conviction and his sureness about his assessment of relative military power confirmed Pearson's growing pessimism about British policy. It was an evening he was not to forget. But in spite of his own conversion to the view that appeasement would not stop Hitler, Pearson confided to friends that the Munich settlement left him with a feeling of schizophrenia. "I was humiliated by the surrender to the Nazis and the betrayal of the Czechs," he said, "yet as an individual I felt such an overwhelming sense of relief that war had been postponed that I found it hard in my heart to be too critical of Chamberlain."

Home leave came up for him during the summer of 1939. With his wife and two children he returned to Canada to spend two months with the family of a brother-in-law, Norman Young—later killed at Dieppe as an officer of the Winnipeg Cameron Highlanders—at a cottage on Lac du Bonnet, near Winnipeg. Coming into the nearby town one day for mail and papers, he learned that Hitler had moved against Danzig. "This is it," Pearson told himself.

Leaving his family with their relatives, he departed immediately for Ottawa. He told Undersecretary O. D. Skelton he wanted to return to London. Skelton agreed—if Pearson wanted to cut short his leave, he had no objection. But Pearson wanted to fly. "I may not even get back before war breaks out," he told Skelton. No Canadian government official had at that time flown the Atlantic; Pan American had just instituted flights with its big flying boats, the first of the clippers. After a bit of an argument, Pearson was authorized to fly, and taking a Canadian government plane to New York, he transferred to a clipper for Southampton. His fellow passengers were nearly all German and Polish reserve officers going back home.

Before Pearson left, however, Skelton thought he should have a talk with the prime minister. Pearson went out to King's country estate, Kingsmere, in the Gatineau hills of Quebec just across the Ottawa River, for leave-taking. "You are being panicky about this," King told him. "You should finish your leave. Of course, if you want to go, that's your business, but you're being foolish. There isn't going to be a war." This was only about ten days before the conflict began, but King was not alone in his hope that the crisis would blow over once again.

Insight into Pearson's outlook on his return to London comes from his diary entries of the period. He commented on a speech by Neville Chamberlain: "The speech as it happens got a good reception here but I still maintain it was a mediocre effort. . . . This country needs strong war leadership. It will never get it from the present government." He groused about Ottawa's editing of a speech announcing plans to use Canada as a training ground for commonwealth fliers. "The conception is gigantic, magnificent, but you would never have thought so listening to the accents of Sir Kingsley (Wood). That wasn't his fault, however. It was largely due to Ottawa, which was worried by the magnitude of the plan and wouldn't allow the air minister to mention any of the figures involved.

There's a world of difference between '20,000 pilots a year' and 'many pilots a year.' If all the suggestions from Ottawa had been followed the speech would have been merely milk and water. Some apparently still think there that a war can be conducted in second gear."

He found war propaganda, from both sides, grimly amusing. "I spend half an hour or so these evenings listening to the German broadcasts in English. They are a scream—but they are meant to frighten, not amuse . . . On the other hand, British propaganda is about as bad as it could be because of official reticence." He told how the Ministry of Information had sent Canada House some pictures of the Royal Navy for propaganda use in Canada. A good proportion were of the battleships *Royal Oak* and *Courageous,* both of which had been sunk by the Germans. "Not a happy choice of the Navy in action."

On November 10, 1939, he wrote: "Late tonight I was dragged out of bed by the *Daily Mail* to confirm a report that the Canadian minister had advised all Canadians to leave Belgium. I said I knew nothing about it. I felt like adding that the only communication we have had from our Legation in Brussels during these trying times was a telegram asking us to purchase six dozen brass buttons for footmen's uniforms with the Canadian coat of arms on them."

Sardonically he wrote of his own entry into the propaganda war when a visiting Canadian cabinet member was asked by the B.B.C. to broadcast to Germany. "I have been writing him a speech that will make the Germans, if any of them brave the penalties of listening to foreign broadcasts, want to abandon the war as hopeless. It's a nice mixture of bricks and kindness, with much emphasis on how Canada, more in sorrow than in anger, is going to throw all the weight of her huge strength—especially her economic strength—on the side of the Allies till victory is assured."

He told about negotiations to sell Canadian wheat to Britain; Canada wanted ninety-three cents a bushel while the British thought seventy-three cents, the world price, amounted to highway robbery. But the "wheat war," he commented, "has been a picnic compared to another struggle centered at Canada House this week—namely the battle over who will run the Canadian Women's war work." The opposing factions were Mrs. Massey and "certain titled gentlewomen who have been accustomed to command the Canadian Women's Club, and who have viewed Mrs. Massey's rise to recent command of the Beaver Club with a jaundiced eye . . . I'm trying hard to keep out of this scrap." A subsequent entry recorded that Mrs. Massey lost one contest when the titled ladies physically raided the office and seized the files. "Nothing but a company of anti-tank troops could have prevented those embattled gentlewomen wreaking their wrath on Mrs. Massey's official possessions which they had decided belonged to them by virtue of their position as executives of the Canadian Women's Club."

On December 25 he wrote: "The first Christmas of the war, and a pall—spiritual and physical—over everything. . . . My telephone call to Winnipeg, arranged after much wangling, was the high water mark of the day for me and it was almost too exciting to be satisfactory."

Ottawa's lack of response to requests for instructions continued to annoy him. On January 8, 1940, he wrote: "Benes came in to see the High Commissioner this morning officially —to establish relations on behalf of the Czech Slovak committee now recognized by France. We knew this was in the air and had cabled Ottawa, asking whether we should receive him—as, if we did, it constituted in a sense, recognition. As Ottawa didn't reply, the High Commissioner was nervous as to what to do, but I didn't see any danger in meeting Benes and advised to that effect."

A few days later he noted: "The Prime Minister has demanded from the High Commissioner the preliminary draft submission to the King on the declaration of war. Mr. Massey understandably has resolved not to give it up without an argument. They are both 'smoke screening' the real issue—which is merely who will retain such an historic souvenir. The Prime Minister says it is required in Ottawa for the Archives. The High Commissioner counters by saying that on the signing of the later and more formal submission which had been mailed from Ottawa, the early one is of no importance—indeed that it should be destroyed—as the King's private secretary himself suggested. We'll now wait until Mr. King finally says he wants the document for himself."

Two entries recorded the effects of war. January 10, 1940: "Two yellow air raid warnings today. The Germans are getting closer—playing about the Thames estuary. But no one worries much now. We don't even carry our gas masks, except the soldiers who have to."

In January Mrs. Pearson arranged to join her husband in London, leaving the children in Winnipeg. A friend, Jack Patteson, London representative of the Canadian Pacific Railroad, advised Pearson that she should postpone her sailing. Pearson asked External Affairs to cable him what liner she finally took, but got no reply. Patteson, however, got the information and Pearson wrote on February 6: "I was glad my wife was not on the ocean when I read my *Times* this morning because the first headline that met my eye was 'CPR Liner Torpedoed.'"

At the end of the Ottawa communications line in front-line London, the view of Mackenzie King continued to be rather critical. After the death of Lord Tweedsmuir, the governor general of Canada, Massey thought it would be appropriate to have a memorial service at Westminster Abbey, and cabled King, asking him to consult Lady Tweedsmuir to see if it was agreeable to her. Pearson quoted King's reply: "I should wholly approve if undertaken by authorities in the United Kingdom at their expense, but if expenditures by the Canadian government were involved, it would be necessary to consult my colleagues." Pearson commented: "I hate to think that a war time cabinet has to spend time discussing matters of this kind." Mr. King reported by cable the following day that the cabinet had turned down the expenditure but approved the service if the Canadians in London financed it on their own. He explained: "You will realize further difficulty that would be involved in any apparently official recognition of a state church," he added, explaining also that his previous reference to the cost was "not because the expenditure was of any significance in itself but because it implied that the service was an official ceremony held on behalf of the government of Canada."

On another occasion Pearson reported long telegrams from King about the appointment of the Earl of Athlone as successor to Lord Tweedsmuir and simultaneously a phone call from Tommy Lascelles at Buckingham Palace, asking whether something could be done about King's telegraphic verbosity. "He complained that they had received the other day an 11-

page telegram from him [the prime minister] in secret cypher, which meant that it had to be decoded at night, that the use of the cypher in such a long telegram was prejudiced, and that it took hours of work on the part of their staff. He said there was nothing in the telegram that couldn't have been sent in one page of ordinary code. We have had the same trouble here, namely Ottawa's using of the cypher in unimportant messages. It is a very ticklish thing to bring to the attention of the Prime Minister, however, who may be naturally inclined to think that anything he sends from Ottawa is of enough significance that it should go in secret cypher. I tried to draft a tactful telegram gently suggesting that for long messages of this kind the ordinary code was adequate."

With the advent of war the Canadian high commissioner's office in London went, of course, on a war footing. The top staff members alternated as duty officers, taking turns in standing by for evening calls if the watch personnel reported news requiring emergency action. Code clerks were summoned if a cable came in marked "most immediate" or carried a certain code designation, and the appropriate officer was notified, no matter what the hour was.

London was hit by an intensifying series of German air raids. One night Pearson, as duty officer, got a call from the code clerk at his flat in Roehampton.

"Well, Mr. Pearson, I've got one of the 'most immediates' in," he reported, "and this is going to make you smile. I hope you don't have to come down four miles through the air raid to deal with it."

"If it's a war secret, I'd better come down," Pearson said, "but if it isn't, perhaps you could read it to me, even if it's against the rules."

"Oh, I can read it to you," said the clerk.

It was from Mr. Mackenzie King. He had heard that in the previous night's raid Westminster Hall, part of the House of Commons, had been damaged by Nazi bombs. One of Mr. King's hobbies was to collect old ruins for his Kingsmere estate, and he wanted someone from Canada House to see if he could get a few stones from the historic building in which the British Parliament had developed.

Dutifully, Pearson visited the works office next day and arranged to have two stones from the rubble retrieved, crated, and shipped to Ottawa, although officials at the office received the request with something less than enthusiasm. "I can't blame them," Pearson remarked. "They're not worrying about the exportation of ruins, they're worrying about the creation of ruins." It was characteristic of King that he could intrude trivial, personal requests at times of national crisis. J. W. Pickersgill, in *The Mackenzie King Record,* records an instance when King, noting that lieutenant governors of the provinces took precedence over cabinet ministers at the funeral of Minister of National Defense Norman Rogers, took time during the week when France was collapsing to dictate a memo to King George VI asking that the table of precedence be changed to reverse the ranking.

A change of tone came over Pearson's entries when the "phony war" ended and the Germans began their invasion of France, though he was still capable of mordantly light-hearted comment. For May 10, 1940, his entry was: "Well, the war has at last really begun. I nearly always listen to the 8 o'clock news on the radio while reclining peacefully in bed. This morning, however, I couldn't hear it clearly, the reason being that the Germans were on the move in Belgium and Holland—over France and possibly over England—and therefore the BBC had weakened its wavelength. I am writing this at noon and everything is still indistinct." He noted that the Whitsun holiday had been canceled throughout the country. "That, I think, is the most impressive indication I have received yet that this country is really getting serious about the war. When the Englishman gives up his Whitsun he has really got down to it. Another indication that the country is waking up to what it is up against is that at long last Mr. Chamberlain is out and Churchill is in."

The fall of France convinced Pearson that his wife ought to go home. It looked as though the Nazis would invade Britain almost any day.

Mrs. Pearson was determined to stay and see it through, but was finally prevailed on to leave when Pearson got together with General H. D. G. Crerar, then head of military headquarters, and Hume Wrong, a fellow external-affairs officer who had come in to London from Geneva to help at Canada House. The men presented a united front to their wives about getting out of danger's path. "Think of the children," the husbands argued. Finally the three ladies arranged to return by ship—actually as dangerous, at the time, with German submarines taking a heavy toll of Atlantic shipping, as facing London's air raids. Their husbands saw them off for Liverpool. But Mrs. Wrong, though she boarded the ship with the others, quietly had a porter take her trunk back down the gangway and took a train back to London. The two other wives were furious when they discovered her defection, feeling they had been betrayed. Mrs. Wrong stuck it out in London, taking care of Pearson and General Crerar in their flat and later serving as an air-raid warden in London's East End, through some of the war's worst bombings.

Among Pearson's many diary entries concerning duties performed in connection with war plans was this one, in February, 1941: "I attended a meeting of the British delegations to the Atlantic bases conference this morning. The conference is not going very well, as the Americans are taking advantage of British necessities and exploiting the situation, or so it seems, in order to prepare the way for ultimate acceptance of their sovereignty over the territories in question. The colonies see this and are fighting hard against any provisions which would seem to infer that the United States has any sovereign rights in the bases, let alone in the adjacent territory. As a result the conference has become bogged in legal arguments and undoubtedly will have to be lifted to a higher political plane if it is not to break up. Our direct interest, of course, is restricted to Newfoundland. If the United States makes good its claim to certain rights and powers which it is proposing to exercise over Newfoundland, we would find ourselves in a rather difficult position. Unfortunately we are only observers at the conference and cannot take a very active part. So far all that we have done is to keep Ottawa informed of what has been going on and of the difficulties and changes of the situation. In return we have not had a single word from them. If they are not worried, I don't know why we should be!

"The Bermudans, three in number, are particularly apprehensive as they see their colony virtually disappearing from the British Empire. That is, in fact, what this agreement ultimately will mean. It is the beginning of the end so far as the British American colonies are concerned."

Pearson probably would have stayed at his post in London for the war's duration had it not been that Undersecretary Skelton died suddenly of a heart attack. On March 29 King sent Massey a cable recalling Pearson to Ottawa. He told Massey: "I feel Pearson should be brought back to Ottawa, probably as additional assistant undersecretary. I have taken some time to come to this conclusion because I appreciate to the full what his assistance means to you and difficulty there may be under present conditions in finding a suitable replacement for him on your staff. Pearson's long separation from his family is an additional reason why he should be given opportunity of returning to Canada. The imperative reason however is . . . to obtain best possible assistance for [Norman] Robertson, the acting undersecretary of state for external affairs."

Pearson was of two minds about the transfer. "I ought, of course, to be both excited and delighted at the thought of getting back to Ottawa," he wrote. "But I don't quite feel that way about it. If it were not for the family being there I just wouldn't go. But that is such a strong inducement that I find myself torn between conflicting emotions. One hates to leave London at this time, and the only real compensation— apart from family considerations—would be that the work I was going back to was more important than that which I am now doing, from the point of view of the war. That may be the case, but I am not quite sure. Like so many telegrams from Mr. King there is a good deal that one can read in between the lines and much that is not clear cut and explicit."

Robertson ranked junior in the career service compared to Pearson and to a number of others, but he was on the spot and was King's personal choice. Knowing that Pearson would be disappointed at being passed over for the top career job, King wrote Pearson explaining the facts of the situation, praising his work in London, and suggesting that in view of the tense time he had gone through in the beleaguered capital it was time he came home to be with his family.

As a result, Pearson returned to Ottawa in June, 1941. The worst raids of all occurred shortly before he left; the Germans were throwing everything they had into their attacks on the British Isles before withdrawing some of their air strength for the impending strike against Russia. A diary entry of April 16 records Pearson's feelings at the time: "What a night! Got in from Star Cross and did a desultory day's work as I was still feeling rotten. At 5:30 suggested to Charles [Ritchie, now Canadian ambassador in Washington] we spend the lovely spring evening dining at the Old Bell at Hurley. It was lovely there, but we came back to inferno. I spent one of the worst nights of my life—fires, whistling bombs, house shaking, ambulances and fire engines racing. The morning after was welcome, God knows, but the west end was a grim sight and traffic was, of course, all tied up. Park Lane was littered with glass and debris. Piccadilly was closed, and so was the Strand. Buildings were down everywhere—it was a sad sight ... all the staff got to work in spite of difficulties. The girls in the office were calm and collected—no trace of dismay or fear."

Pearson still remembers his relief on arriving in Lisbon on the way home, with its contrast to London's tensions. The city was brightly lit and there was plenty of food in the shops. To reporters who asked why the Nazi air raids had suddenly seemed to abate, he quipped: "As soon as they learned I had left London they decided to slack off."

By this time Mackenzie King was more impressed with the diplomat he had thought "too panicky" two years before. Pickersgill's *The Mackenzie King Record* cites this excerpt from King's diary of the period:

"Had a talk with Pearson, who has just returned from England. Very interesting conversation on the whole situation. He spoke of the amazing calm of the people and their determination. Feels a great concern about what may arise out of Vichy. Thinks Dupuy over-optimistic. Brought his latest report to me. Reported his readiness to begin work at once . . . Very modest, unassuming. He is going to be valuable to Robertson."

Pearson found Ottawa buzzing with gossip over the fact that King had passed him over, as well as others, in naming a new undersecretary. He was a more popular officer than Robertson, and his seniority was an added point in his favor. All over town the cocktail-party talk was that Mike should have had the job; tongues were wagging as they can wag only in a small capital where those in diplomatic circles all know each other. The gossips even speculated whether under the circumstances Pearson would be able to work for Robertson.

It happened that Pearson was booked to speak to the Ottawa Canadian Club, a luncheon organization, immediately after his return. Members were eager to hear firsthand about the bombings of Britain. After he was introduced, but before he began his talk, he took a minute to say that since his arrival he had heard much gossip about his appointment as assistant to Robertson.

"I want it known right now," said Pearson, "that I think Norman Robertson's appointment was an excellent one and that I will be glad to work with him. If anyone can take Dr.

Skelton's place, he is the man." By meeting the gossip head-on, he put an end to it overnight.

He did not stay long in Ottawa, however. He was still Robertson's assistant at the time of Pearl Harbor. Though it was Sunday, he was at the office when he got the news, from someone who had heard the radio. He recalls he felt a tremendous relief, thinking that now there was no doubt who would win the war; although he had never believed Britain would give in and lose the war, it was difficult at that stage to see how she *could* win. At home Mrs. Pearson and twelve-year-old Patsy had heard the radio reports of the Japanese attack, too. Shortly afterward a caller stopped at the house: General Crerar, who was by then chief of the general staff, and who had been out for a Sunday afternoon walk in Rockcliffe Park, unaware of the tremendous turn the war had taken. Mrs. Pearson sent Patsy downstairs to talk to the General until she could come down. After exhausting the weather as a topic, Patsy remarked:

"Isn't it awful about the Japanese bombing Pearl Harbor?"

"What!" exploded the General. "They haven't!"

"Oh, yes, they have," Patsy told him. Crerar paced the floor, muttering, "I don't believe it!" and then walked out the front door without further ado.

6

Lunch with Truman

IT WAS shortly afterward that Leighton McCarthy, the Canadian minister to Washington, informed Mackenzie King he would like to have Pearson assigned to the legation as number-two man. Pearson was not well acquainted with McCarthy, but the minister apparently was impressed with the record he was making in the service, and King was glad to honor his friend's request. Pearson's rank was counselor, soon raised to minister-counselor, and when McCarthy left he was made head of the mission as minister. Later the mission was raised to embassy status and Pearson became the first Canadian ambassador to the U.S.

In Washington, Pearson became one of the most popular foreign diplomats. He made friends easily and developed a wide acquaintance with members of the press. James Reston, then diplomatic correspondent and later bureau chief of *The New York Times,* he had known in London. Pearson discovered that informal relations with the press could be a big help in his work, keeping him up to date on Washington affairs on a level different from official life. He used to attend baseball games with Reston and others or sit around the National Press Club, enjoying casual conversation with various correspondents.

Life in Washington was mercifully free of the bombardments of London, but it was a crowded time for Pearson. The United States and Britain set up a great number of combined boards to co-ordinate their war effort, and on many of them Canada was represented too. This kept Pearson involved in an endless round of meetings that related to almost all phases of the conduct and planning of the war. Lieutenant General Maurice A. Pope, who was chairman of the Canadian joint-staff mission to Washington in 1943, recounts in his memoirs, *Soldiers and Politicians,* that on one occasion in a report to his headquarters on a subject in which both military and civilian authorities were interested, he mentioned, without thinking, that "Mr. Pearson" would be dealing with the same matter in a message of external affairs. Leighton McCarthy happened to see a copy of his dispatch, and called Pope in and ticked him off for seeming to be "unaware that the legation was headed by a quite competent minister." Pope also recalls an occasion in which he sought to get eighteen amendments made to a paper on the disposition of Canadian air strength, and won agreement to twelve. Pearson told him cheerfully: "A batting average of .666 is superlatively good in any league."

Among the boards on which Pearson served was the combined-policy committee, which developed the atomic bomb. He played no part in the program but provided a channel

74

of communication to his government, and he knew what was going on. C. D. Howe, King's production wizard, made frequent trips to Washington, and Pearson had chores of various kinds assisting him.

In Washington, as in London, Pearson did personal errands for Mr. King. One, more serious than the request for stones from Westminster Hall, involved seeing President Roosevelt in July, 1943.

The Allies were preparing to land in Italy and Canadian troops were to take part in their first major involvement in the invasion. King learned from his defense minister, J. L. Ralston, that the communiqué being prepared for release after the landings referred only to forces of the U.S. and Great Britain. He cabled Vincent Massey in London to see if it could not be changed to include mention of the Canadian troops, but got back a message saying that "for reasons of security" the British were doubtful that Canada's participation could be mentioned.

King fired off cables of protest both to London and Washington and in addition decided to have Pearson, who was temporarily chargé d'affaires in Washington during McCarthy's absence, see President Roosevelt about it. King telephoned Pearson and asked him to do it immediately—since the landings were imminent and the communiqué was to be released at midnight. It was then about 5 P.M.

"President Roosevelt is giving a dinner for General de Gaulle tonight," Pearson told him. "I'm not sure I can get in unless you prepare the way for me."

King said he would call Harry Hopkins about it. Soon Pearson got a call from Hopkins; he had heard from King about Pearson's urgent need to see the President, but he did not know what it was all about. Pearson explained King's concern that Canadian morale would suffer unless some recognition were given Canada in the communiqué, for the whole Canadian division was in on the landing that was to be the first step in the reconquest of Europe.

Hopkins said he thought the request was reasonable, and urgent, and he would try to arrange the meeting, but he asked Pearson to come to see him first.

On arriving at the White House Pearson was taken up in an elevator to a second-floor room where Hopkins and his wife, Louise Macy, were waiting. He knew if he convinced Hopkins of the importance of the communiqué to Canada it would help convince Roosevelt. He made his pitch as strong as possible on the basis of Canada's need to let the public know that at long last her troops were getting into major allied action.

After they had been talking for a while, President Roosevelt came in and Pearson repeated his argument. The President asked a few questions and sought Hopkins' advice. Finally he said: "I think we ought to do this for the Canadians."

"But how can you do it if the communiqué is to come out in a few hours?" Pearson inquired.

"Don't worry, it will be seen to," Roosevelt reassured him.

Pearson returned to the embassy and telephoned Norman Robertson in Ottawa to let him know the mission had been carried out. He worked in his office until nearly midnight, then called for his car and drove up Connecticut Avenue toward his home. On the car radio a dance band was playing. Suddenly it was interrupted for an announcement: British, American, and Canadian forces had invaded Europe.

Pearson's car was just pulling up to his house. As he got out he was told there was a telephone call: "Ottawa wants to speak to you." Mr. King was very happy over his performance.

Pearson found Washington had bureaucratic foibles of its own, different from London's but related. A Canadian friend arrived to attend some hush-hush meetings on wireless interception of enemy messages. "At the first meeting," Pearson recorded in his diary, "the Americans glared at him suspiciously and refused to talk, as he had not been cleared by some mysterious authority known as 'G.2,' although they knew he was chairman of the Canadian committee doing most confidential work in the same field. Some of the security arrangements in this capital are laughable in their intensity." He was amused by the first air-raid alarm he experienced, which came during a luncheon with several officials: "We had to remain in the restaurant for an extra half hour. It is hard to take this sort of thing seriously, but I remember how we were inclined to laugh at it in London in the summer of 1939. Like everything else, of course, they have made the various alarm signals here as complicated as possible. In any event, if there were a real raid, nobody would pay any attention to them as everybody would be out on the street having a look."

His initial and inaccurate judgment of United States postwar policy made him suspect the country would revert to isolationism as after the first world war. On February 8, 1943, he wrote: "All the talk is of peace these days, with the Germans apparently retreating headlong before the Russians. Unfortunately, thoughts of victory in Washington are accompanied by a recrudescence of political strife. My own view is that American foreign policy after this war is going to be along

77

the same line as it was after the last. The fact of the matter is that most Americans are natural isolationists, and only international co-operators in an emergency. We are in for a sticky time." He was soon to see and admit he had been wrong.

On March 8 he told of having been summoned by Assistant Secretary of State Adolph Berle to be handed a preliminary draft of a U.S. proposal for United Nations postwar financial stabilization, on which Canadian comments were invited. "Getting into difficulties in my efforts to maintain a discussion on the highest levels of international banking and currency, I tried to switch him over to talk about a United Nations conference," Pearson wrote. "I suggested that with all these technical subjects now looming up for general discussion, such a conference should be held, which, if it did nothing else, could set up United Nations committees to consider them. Such committees would thereby derive their authority from the United Nations and not from one of President Roosevelt's press conferences. Berle thought it was a good idea, but felt that political considerations here might make it difficult. He was inclined to think that from a practical point of view it was better to proceed with scattered *ad hoc* United Nations discussions."

During a visit to Washington by Anthony Eden, Pearson noted: "Eden's visit seemed to be going pretty well, though he is having some difficulty removing [Cordell] Hull's suspicion about British policy in North Africa, and he is learning that the Japs are the Americans' first enemy and that therefore China—quite apart from Madame Chiang Kai-shek's charm—looms large with them. Eden is making a good impression on people here generally . . . He seems to have developed more confidence and assurance than he had when I knew him in London. He is leaving for Ottawa next Tuesday, by plane, and I received a telegram from the P.M. on Friday telling me to be in Ottawa at the same time. I immediately phoned Oliver Harvey to see if I could have a ride on Mr. Churchill's special plane, which is carrying the Eden party. I had visions of taking a bath in Churchill's special bathtub (this plane is the only one that seems to possess one) high over New York. I might even pull the plug over the Empire State Building. Unfortunately, Lew Douglas has pinched the only available place on the plane. Canadian-U.S. relations are consequently worsened and I am going by train."

Pearson began to change his opinion about America's postwar attitude after he attended a luncheon of the Institute of Pacific Relations at which Undersecretary of State Sumner Welles spoke. "I was enjoying my chicken and preparing myself for the oratorical treat which was to follow," he recorded, "when the chairman, Carter, slipped over to tell me he was going to call on me, as Canada had been the host at the last IPR conference at Mont Tremblant. That was a shock. I did not enjoy the chicken any more. However, I managed to hold forth for about five minutes on Canada and the Pacific and murmured something about 'a bomb dropped on a Chinese village echoes across the St. Lawrence—that is something we Canadians have learned.' I was surprised to find each subsequent speaker referring to this statement. After it was over, I came to the conclusion that possibly it is better not to be told about speeches you have to make until you make them! It saves a lot of preliminary sweating.

"Sumner Welles was very good, making a plea for postwar collective security and an international police force. He is preaching the pure doctrine these days, and I hope he will be listened to. There seems to be more possibility of this now than six months ago. At the moment, the isolationists seem to be retreating in Congress." At about the same time, Pearson attended a luncheon at which "an American journalist back from China, Alsop, talked about his experiences. He was extraordinarily good. Without any illusions about that part of the world, he was emphatic that if the United States did not jump in and play a big part in the international organization of the Pacific and convince the Chinese that they were willing to accept responsibility for peace in that area, the Russians and the Chungking people would come together. He felt that the Chinese realized that they could not stand alone."

Pearson's Washington diary contains one entry illustrating perfectly a diplomat's need to be aware of the nuances in official telegrams and how to read between the lines of communications. It concerned a visit to Washington by Winston Churchill. The entry says:

"Mr. Churchill arrived on Tuesday evening. The same evening about 10 o'clock Norman [Robertson] phoned me from Ottawa to say that a teletype was on the way, inviting Mr. Churchill to Ottawa, and could I get it down to the White House at once. It was perfectly clear that Norman was trying to tell me that if Mr. Churchill did not find it possible to go to Ottawa, Mr. King was willing to accept an invitation to Washington—more than willing. I was asked somehow to convey this impression to Mr. Churchill that night or first thing next morning.

"I got Ronnie Campbell on the phone, and he suggested I get hold of General Ismay, who is very close to Churchill. Ismay, however, thought that it had much better be done through Churchill's principal private secretary, Rowan. I got Rowan on the phone early the next morning, read him the telegram from Ottawa, which I said would follow by hand; asked him to bring it at once to Mr. Churchill's attention, and suggested that a reply before noon would be very greatly appreciated. I hinted that our Parliament in Ottawa would be questioning Mr. King in the afternoon as to whether he had been informed of or invited to the meetings in Washington and that Mr. King would like to have something to say in reply. I also hinted as delicately as I knew how that if Mr. Churchill could not go to Ottawa, Mr. King could possibly come to Washington.

"Rowan was quick to grasp what I was driving at, and he said he would see Mr. Churchill at once. He certainly did his part, because a telegram came back to the Legation for transmission to Mr. King before lunch. It was exactly what we wanted—deep regrets that W.S.C. could not go to Ottawa, with a warm invitation to come to Washington, where 'he (Mr. Churchill) and the President would be delighted to see him.' To make sure that this message would get to Mr. King before the House met, I phoned the Country Club, where our P.M. was giving a luncheon to the President of Bolivia, got Norman away from the luncheon, and gave him the good news. They were all delighted.

"The next day I told Jack Hickerson of the invitation from Mr. Churchill, and he was annoyed because Churchill and not the President had invited Mr. King. Apparently he got busy, because the next day a telegram was sent to our P.M. from Mr. Roosevelt somewhat as follows: 'I am delighted to know that you can accept *my* invitation. Please come to the White House immediately on arrival on Wednesday.' Mr.

King must be flattered to have the two great men fighting over his body."

During King's visit Pearson "got the P.M. to call at the Legation this afternoon and meet all the staff. He does this sort of thing very well. He was to have gone also to the Annex and to the Joint Staff building, but, though everybody there was on parade and remained expectant for an hour or so, the P.M. himself never turned up. Instead, he drove off to see an old friend."

After the Canadian legation was raised to embassy status—Roosevelt had proposed it to Prime Minister King on that trip—and Pearson became ambassador, Pearson was obliged to make ceremonial calls on Washington officials. By chance he called on Chief Justice Harlan Fisk Stone at the Supreme Court and on Vice-President Harry Truman at the Senate Office Building on the same morning. In his report to Ottawa he wrote: "The Vice President was very affable and informal. In contrast to my reaction in the outer office of the Supreme Court, which was very formal and dignified, my introduction to the Vice President was as casual as it was friendly. I was taken in hand by a pleasant but rather seedy-looking individual, who was chewing a 'Milky Way,' and ushered into the Vice Presidential chamber in very much the same genial but off-hand manner as a visitor to the local Rotary Club. I never did get the name or the position of my introducer, but I gathered he was one of the Vice President's staff." While he was talking with Truman one of the latter's Senate cronies, Carl Hatch, wandered in. "Both gentlemen closed my visit by emphatic statements that Canada was the great friend of the United States," Pearson reported, "and if only all countries were as reasonable and neighbourly as we were, how much better the world would be. As I have said many times before, this approach is all very gratifying, but makes it somewhat more difficult for us to impress on our friends here that there are, nevertheless, Canadian-American problems, the solution of which is sometimes not made easier by the American tendency to treat us as another State of the Union, but one without congressional representation; a kind of external District of Columbia."

Toward the end of the war Pearson began to get involved in the various plans being made for peace. In addition to following the pre-United Nations conversations that took place at Dumbarton Oaks, and working on drafting the UN charter at the founding conference in San Francisco, he took part in the postwar planning of the Food and Agriculture Organization and the United Nations Relief and Rehabilitation Administration. He found he was spending as much time in such activity as on strictly Canadian affairs.

It was then that he first began to attract international attention. His work with UNRRA put him in contact first with Herbert Lehman and later with Fiorello LaGuardia; he had long been known to Dean Acheson, and at San Francisco he got to know Senator Arthur Vandenberg.

One postwar incident stands out in his mind as clearly as the London dinner with Churchill. It involved lunch with Harry Truman aboard the presidential yacht, *Williamsburgh.*

Shortly after the dropping of the atom bomb on Hiroshima had brought victory over Japan, British Prime Minister Clement Attlee made a visit to Washington to talk over with Truman what Allied policy should be with respect to the transcendent new power that had been unleashed on the world. Mackenzie King came on behalf of Canada, which had supplied the uranium with which the bomb had been built. After a Saturday-afternoon session at the White House it was decided to continue the discussions next day aboard the yacht.

Two principals from each of the three countries, plus a few technical men, boarded the *Williamsburgh* at eleven o'clock on Sunday for a cruise down the Potomac. Truman was accompanied by his secretary of state, James F. Byrnes, Attlee by his Washington ambassador, Lord Halifax, and King by Pearson. They went below deck to a small cabin and sat around a small table covered with green baize—where Truman liked to play poker on more relaxed cruises—and Truman announced:

"Now I'm going to ask everybody at this table to say what he thinks should be done about this terrible new power we have discovered."

Pearson, quite overwhelmed by the magnitude of the discussion and the presence of the heads of government, remembers his first thought was one of panic at having to speak up in such company. But he said he thought the only hope for saving the world from the potential of evil in the bomb was by internationalizing it. "It was not a very original observation," he said later, "but it was an obvious one, and a simple one." The fact was that the thinking of all the conferees ran along the same line.

When the meeting broke up for lunch Truman and Byrnes had their favorite drink—bourbon and branch water—and the atmosphere became rather convivial, rather to the dismay of Attlee and Halifax, as well as King, who was virtually a teetotaler. But after lunch they returned to the discussion— how could internationalization be accomplished? All afternoon the problem was hashed over while the *Williamsburgh* cruised down the Potomac.

Just before 6 P.M. Truman interrupted. "This is Sunday," he said. "Drew Pearson goes on the air at six o'clock with his predictions of things to come. I've got to listen to him." With Attlee and King not quite knowing what to make of it, the group gathered around a radio in the next cabin to listen to Drew Pearson's weekly predictions. Afterward, the job of writing a communiqué on the two-day meeting was turned over to Mike Pearson, Vannevar Bush, and one of Attlee's men. Pearson never recalls the subsequent evolution of the Baruch plan for international control of the atom—blocked by the Soviet Union when it was presented to the UN—without remembering the bourbon lunch and the Drew Pearson broadcast that interrupted the three-power conference where the plan originated.

Shortly afterward Pearson got his first intimation of a political future. He was on an UNRRA trip with LaGuardia in Europe. They had visited Poland for several days, seeking to determine what that devastated country's relief needs would be, and were about to leave for Minsk in Byelorussia when Pearson got a telegram from King asking him to meet him in Paris. King took him out for a ride one evening in a horse-drawn carriage through the Bois de Boulogne and said he planned to recall Pearson from Washington and appoint him undersecretary of state for external affairs. He mentioned in that connection that the post could lead to Pearson's entering politics.

"You're cut out for politics," King told him.

Pearson's reaction was prompt and negative. He was enjoying his ambassadorial post in Washington. He told King frankly he had no intention of becoming a politician.

"Oh well, you wait," said King. "You think about it."

When Pearson finally left Washington in October, 1946, his friend Scotty Reston wrote in *The New York Times:* "His main rule was informality. When he came here first in 1942 he joined a softball team that played against men from the State Department on Sunday afternoons. He lived in a little house off Connecticut Avenue where he entertained to the limit of his expense account, which was not much of a limit, and saw Congressmen and newspaper reporters with as much regularity as he saw other diplomats.

"He won the respect, confidence, and affection of a remarkably wide range of persons in most phases of Washington life. He carried this same informality into the discussions leading up to the formation of the United Nations. He fought actively against the veto in private conversations during the Dumbarton Oaks conference and argued against it further at San Francisco . . . Washington is certainly not happy to see him go. After the melancholy catalogue of events in the field of foreign affairs these last few years, few serious officials have been able to work incessantly on the problem of peace without losing either their perspective or their sense of humor or both. Mr. Pearson has managed to do that, and has helped a few others do the same. And it is an accomplishment that official Washington is not likely to forget for quite a while."

7

NATO's Canadian Root

THE END of the war signaled changes in command in most capitals of the western alliance, and Ottawa was no exception. Prime Minister Mackenzie King had been his own foreign minister throughout the conflict; he thought it was time to give that part of the job to someone else. For wartime service in his cabinet he had drafted a prominent and respected French Canadian lawyer, Louis St. Laurent, as his minister of justice. Now he wanted St. Laurent to take over the portfolio of external affairs. Although St. Laurent had enlisted for the duration only, he agreed to stay on in the new post—and, as it turned out, eventually to succeed King as Liberal leader and prime minister.

In almost any field of government activity, no matter how hard the minister works, his top career deputy invariably works harder, and this truism applied to Norman Robertson, the undersecretary of state for external affairs. He was worn out by the load of work he had carried and the continuous tension it entailed and deserved a lighter assignment that would give him some measure of rest. Accordingly, Lester Pearson was called in from the embassy in Washington to take over his duties.

Thus Pearson's promotion to top civil-service rank in the career he entered in 1928 coincided with the entry of a new minister; each brought a fresh approach to problems facing Canada in its external relations, and the problems themselves were of a kind much different from those with which their predecessors had been required to wrestle. War requires one course of action, peace another. The world's statesmen faced the job of picking up the pieces left after history's most devastating war and constructing from them a structure in which nations could hope for an enduring peace.

Working together, St. Laurent and Pearson established a mutual rapport and respect that was the foundation of Pearson's subsequent success as a diplomat. St. Laurent developed a profound confidence in his undersecretary, without which Pearson could not have operated as effectively as he did. Pearson, on his part, grew in admiration for the thoughtful, dignified minister for whom he was working. It was not entirely the result of their thinking along the same lines, which they generally did. But when they did disagree, they were able to talk out differences in their viewpoints and reach agreement. Pearson was always able to act in the confident knowledge that whatever course of action they decided on would be fully backed up by his superior.

This priceless asset for a subordinate official carried over later, when St. Laurent became prime minister and Pearson succeeded him as minister for external affairs. In the privacy of the St. Laurent cabinet, the members knew that when Pearson spoke he had the prime minister's backing. St. Laurent usually deferred to the judgment of his trade minister, C. D. Howe, on domestic matters and to Pearson on international affairs. The fact that Pearson confined himself to his own special field tended to smooth his cabinet relationships and made his position effective.

As ambassador to Washington, Pearson had witnessed the origins of the western effort to create a peaceful postwar world, beginning with the conversations at Dumbarton Oaks. Like others involved in the great renewal of effort to build a system of law and order, he had hoped that the co-operation of the great powers that had enabled them to win victory in the war would carry over into co-operation in peacetime. But it quickly became apparent that Soviet Russia was not disposed to make the concessions toward compromise that inevitably had to be made if the conflicting aspirations for freedom and self-government of people all over the world were to be settled in any kind of satisfactory framework. Stalin exhibited firm determination to hold under tight communist domination every inch of territory conquered by the Red Armies.

One can disapprove of such a dog-in-the-manger attitude and still understand that, human nature being what it is, a barbaric despot of Stalin's make-up would act as he did. But when it became apparent that Stalin's greed was still not satisfied and that Russia intended to extend its conquests, western statesmen were faced with the problem of what to do about it. The profoundly disturbing demonstration of Russia's intentions in this respect was the take-over of Czechoslovakia. Being, like Canada, the small neighbor of a great power, Czechoslovakia had had no choice but to ally herself with Russia after the war, striving at the same time to keep such democratic traditions as she could. But this was not enough for Russia. She was not satisfied until she had Czechoslovakia completely under her thumb.

Russia's take-over of Czechoslovakia brought a finality of disillusion to statesmen of democratic countries that is universally credited with prompting formation of the North Atlantic Treaty Organization.

What is not generally known is that Canada was the first nation publicly to propose such an alliance. No complex international organization such as NATO can burgeon into life without having many roots, but it is a matter of record that the first of these roots appeared in the soil of Canada. It occurred in a speech to the House of Commons by Louis St. Laurent, then foreign minister, a speech largely drafted for him by his undersecretary, Lester Pearson.

The occasion was consideration by the House on April 29, 1948, of spending estimates of the Department of External Affairs. Annually each department submits its policies to Parliament for approval, and the occasion calls for what the diplomats like to call a *"tour d'horizon"* in which the minister reviews how the world looks from Canada's vantage point.

In that year's review St. Laurent spoke with somber words about what had just happened in Czechoslovakia, which he described as "a frightening case history of communist totalitarianism in action" and well worth careful study.

"The Nazis were well aware," said St. Laurent, "that in conquering Czechoslovakia they were striking a formidable blow at world democracy. The communist dictators of today are equally conscious of the importance of the Czechoslovak democratic tradition in the western world. When the Czechoslovaks were forced by outside pressure to withdraw their acceptance of the invitation to participate in the discussions of the Marshall Plan in Paris last September, it was clear that Czechoslovakia was not to be permitted to act as a bridge between west and east.

"It has now become apparent to what lengths communist governments will go in preventing co-operation between the free and democratic west and the totalitarian governments of Eastern Europe. The Czechs had loyally lived up to their obligations as members of the Soviet bloc. They were a threat to no one. They were steadily and sturdily rebuilding their economy on a basis of democratic socialism. Yet their liberties have been ruthlessly wiped out by a Soviet-inspired communist fifth column.

"Those in each free nation who love freedom should draw the clear lesson of the tragedy of Czechoslovakia. That lesson is that it is impossible to cooperate with communists. They do not want cooperation. They want domination. Communists will pretend to cooperate with non-communists just as long as it is in their interests to do so. But once they are in a position to seize power, they will seize it and will then discard or destroy their non-communist allies. People in Canada, the United States, France, Italy, and other countries have been long in learning their lesson. Let us hope that they have now learned it well."

This citation of Czechoslovakia as an object lesson led St. Laurent to take note of alarmed reaction in western Europe that had caused five nations to develop plans for a "Western European Union" in which they proposed to band together for their mutual protection. He went on to develop the thought that something of wider scope was needed to protect Canada and her interest in the sound recovery of Europe. "The tragedy of Czechoslovakia in September, 1938, and March, 1939, was a prelude to war," he said. "The tragedy of Czechoslovakia in February, 1948, need not be a prelude to war. It does, however, underline the necessity for the free states of the world to unite their material, their political, and their moral resources to resist direct and indirect totalitarian aggression."

He went on to become more specific. He recalled that in a speech to the United Nations some time earlier he had argued that it was not necessary to contemplate the breakup of the UN or the secession of the Soviet bloc in order to build up a stronger security system within the UN.

"Without sacrificing the universality of the United Nations," he told the House of Commons, "it is possible for the free nations of the world to form their own closer association for collective self-defense under Article 51 of the Charter of the United Nations. Such an association could be created within the United Nations by those free states which are willing to accept more specific and onerous obligations than those contained in the charter, in return for greater national security than the United Nations can now give its members.

"It may be that the free states, or some of them, will soon find it necessary to consult together on how best to establish such a collective security league. It might grow out of the plans for 'Western Union' now maturing in Europe. Its purpose, like that of 'Western Union,' would not merely be negative; it would create a dynamic counter-attraction to communism—the dynamic counter-attraction of a free, prosperous and progressive society as opposed to the totalitarian and re-actionary society of the communist world. The formation of such a defensive group of free states would not be a counsel of despair but a message of hope. It would not mean that we regarded a third world war as inevitable; but that the free democracies had decided that to prevent such a war they would organize so as to confront the forces of communist expansion with an overwhelming preponderance of moral, economic, and military force and with sufficient degree of unity, to ensure that this preponderance of force is so used that the free nations cannot be defeated one by one. No measure less than this will do. We must at all costs avoid the fatal repetition of the history of the prewar years when the Nazi aggressor picked off its victims one by one. Such a process does not end at the Atlantic."

The listing of purposes for what subsequently became NATO as a mobilization of moral, economic, and military power was the hallmark of Pearson's involvement in the thinking that had gone into St. Laurent's speech. From the outset Pearson had wanted NATO to evolve methods of greater economic co-operation and systems of consultation under which more unified political action could bring the moral weight of the western world to bear in the task of peace-keeping. NATO has failed to show development in the nonmilitary fields, though it has not been completely unresponsive.

The great significance for Canada, however, was that a nation that had developed a tradition of avoiding foreign commitments in advance was being asked to turn completely around in the postwar world and accept as basic to its international relations that its best future interests lay in positive partnerships with others to work actively for peace, and for collective defense in war by advance planning.

"I am sure," St. Laurent told the House, "that it is the desire of the people of Canada that Canada should play its full part in creating and maintaining this overwhelming preponderance of moral, economic, and military force and the necessary unity for its effective use. One thing we must constantly keep in mind as we approach this fateful decision is that the Western European democracies are not beggars asking for our charity. They are allies whose assistance we need in order to be able to defend ourselves successfully and our beliefs. Canada and the United States need the assistance of the Western European democracies just as they need ours. The spread of aggressive communist despotism over Western Europe would ultimately almost certainly mean for us war, and war on most unfavorable terms. It is in our national interest to see to it that the flood of communist expansion is held back.

"Our foreign policy today must, therefore, be based on a recognition of the fact that totalitarian communist aggression endangers the freedom and peace of every democratic country, including Canada. On this basis, and pending the strengthening of the United Nations, we should be willing to associate ourselves with other free states in any appropriate collective security arrangements which may be worked out under Articles 51 or 52 of the charter. In the circumstances of the present, the organization of collective defense in this way is the most effective guarantee of peace. The pursuit of this course, steadfastly, unprovocatively, and constructively is our best hope for disproving the gloomy predictions of inevitable war."

A study on "Canada and the United Nations" published in 1956 as one of a series prepared for the Canadian Institute of International Affairs and the Carnegie Endowment for International Peace by F. H. Soward and Edgar McInnis took due note that St. Laurent's speech "was the first public proposal by a cabinet minister in the Atlantic area for an alliance for that region." Before NATO came into being, St. Laurent had moved up to become head of government, and Pearson had replaced him as foreign minister.

In later years, after taking part in more dramatic episodes such as the Suez crisis and in events having more immediate impact, like the Palestine and Korean settlements, Pearson looked back on his role in the formation of NATO as his most important and satisfying. The effectiveness of Canada's voice in the formation process stemmed from the close associations he had built up with Dean Acheson in Washington. The formulation of diplomatic planning for NATO, however, was only half the job; NATO had to be accepted by the Canadian people. This was accomplished by the team of St. Laurent and Pearson, backed by the Conservative opposition leader in the House, George Drew, whom Pearson credited with 100 per cent co-operation once he was convinced NATO was in Canada's national interest.

The creation of NATO was one of four incidents in Pearson's diplomatic career that demonstrates how a nation usually described as a middle power, moving in the company of the great powers, can exert influence out of proportion to its own material strength if it makes use of its opportunities. Almost certainly NATO would have emerged without Canada's initiative, since it represented a basic response to what was recognized on all sides as the clear and present danger of aggressive communism and the inadequacy of existing machinery to ward it off. Canada could have tagged along in the procession. But in this case, as in the three other cases to be examined, Canada took a leading part. It did so because it had among its leaders men willing to take on the job of (in a phrase coined by John Foster Dulles) "waging" peace. Looking back on his diplomatic years later on, it enabled Pearson to tell a friend, "I have always felt that the most important thing I participated in was the formation of NATO. It was not the most exciting thing with which I was associated, nor the most dramatic. It was not even the most *immediately* important thing. But in the long run I think it was the most important."

8

Three Diplomatic Maneuvers

BECAUSE OF THE close association built up between Pearson and St. Laurent, from the standpoint of diplomatic effectiveness Pearson's transition from top-ranking civil
servant in the external-affairs department to policy boss as
minister represented a minimum of change. It made a great
difference politically and for that reason required adjustments
in personal orientation. For example, in 1949, shortly after
he attended the Washington meeting at which the North
Atlantic Treaty was formally signed, and affixed his name as
representative of Canada, he toured his northern Ontario
constituency of Algoma East. One of his supporters reminded
him: "It was a fine thing, Mr. Pearson, to have you signing
that pact with all those big shots in Washington. But remember it won't help you much up here if you don't get us that
new post office."

97

The day he was sworn in as member of the cabinet he telephoned his mother in Toronto.

"Well, Mother," he said, remembering that she had wanted him to be a clergyman, "I'm a minister now."

"I'm delighted, Lester," she replied, "even if it is the second class kind."

It was with considerable reluctance he took the plunge into politics. As a civil servant he had built up a position of personal security and recognition in his profession. Indeed his renown was such that he was often mentioned for international posts. In 1946, at London, when the fledgling United Nations was looking for a secretary-general, Pearson was under informal consideration together with General Dwight D. Eisenhower, Belgium's Paul-Henri Spaak, and Norway's Trygve Lie. U.S. Senator Arthur Vandenberg let it be known that Eisenhower would not consider the job. Spaak took himself out of consideration. The Russians quietly informed Paul Martin, head of the Canadian delegation, that they would object to Pearson, on the ground that anyone from Canada was too closely tied to the United States and Britain to suit them. Thus Lie emerged as the first head of the international secretariat.

When the time came to elect a successor to Lie, Pearson's name again figured in the appointment. He was then president of the General Assembly, serving for the 1952-53 session. Early in 1953, having heard speculation that the Russians might not veto his appointment, he asked a friend to make discreet and informal inquiries of the Russians and the Americans to determine their attitude toward making him secretary-general. The friend reported that the Russians might be willing to accept him.

Pearson found this news disturbing. "I've been taking a high-minded attitude about it," he told the friend, "to the effect that if duty called I would serve. But frankly, I didn't think duty would call." The Russians were so anxious to get rid of Lie, who was serving beyond his term until a successor had been picked, that it seemed they might accept Pearson if the British and Americans insisted on it.

During a trip to Ottawa, Pearson dropped in to see Prime Minister St. Laurent one night after the House session and told him about the situation. "If the Security Council nominates me, I think I should accept," he said. "But if they merely offer the General Assembly two or three names, one of them mine, I would withdraw."

St. Laurent said he would hate to see Pearson leave the cabinet on the eve of an election he was about to call, but agreed that if he was the choice of the Security Council he would have no alternative.

A few days later *The New York Times* carried a front-page story saying the Russians were prepared to accept Pearson as secretary-general. The story worried those of Pearson's friends who were pushing him for the job, as it seemed likely to hinder their effort; but Pearson felt relieved that he might escape having to make the decision. He was content to let events develop as they would.

On March 2 he thought the matter settled when Andrei Vishinsky went out of his way to attack him during a speech in the political committee, charging him with bias. Pearson's supporters, however, refused to give up, and as the maneuvering went on, three names emerged. Russia gave notice of intention to support a member of the Polish delegation, apparently for bargaining purposes; the United States announced support of Carlos Romulo of the Philippines; and Denmark proposed to nominate Pearson. The U.S. delegate, Henry Cabot Lodge, told Pearson that if Romulo failed to get enough votes they would support him, and Pearson replied that whatever the U.S. chose to do in this matter was all right with him.

With the issue coming to a head, Pearson thought it was seemly for him to return to Ottawa until it was settled. By telephone on the evening of March 19 he was informed that the Security Council had voted—under British delegate Gladwyn Jebb's insistence that the matter be settled—and Romulo had received 5 votes, Pearson 9. However, the Russians had vetoed Pearson. This ended his consideration, though it did not solve the problem of Lie's successor. The question was settled when the Russians agreed on Dag Hammarskjold.

After Hammarskjold's death in an airplane crash in the Congo, Pearson was once again brought into the speculation about a successor, but by that time he was too thoroughly committed to his political career to think about it seriously, and he knew in any event nothing had made him more acceptable to the Russians in the interim.

There were other times when he was sought as secretary-general of NATO, in whose affairs he had been so completely involved for so long. That post never carried the same appeal; if he could not serve in the world forum, he preferred to devote his efforts more directly to the service of his own country and accept the responsibilities that went with it. The pull of duty and of Canada was strong. Once, shortly after he had gained world attention, he was asked to head one of the major American educational foundations. It would have meant greater financial reward, and removal from the stress of politics that can be felt in top civil-service jobs as well as in policy posts. He was in New York at the time, and so was Mackenzie King. He and King spent an hour riding around Central Park in a taxicab while they talked it over; Pearson finally decided against it. Years later, after he became prime minister, Pearson told a friend: "When I look back on my career, the most amazing thing is that things just happened. Mr. Diefenbaker said he always had a goal and worked toward it. Nothing like that with me. I was always alert for any opportunities or responsibilities or interesting work, but if I didn't take it on, it didn't worry me. I'd do something else. I have never hewn to any particular line. It was only pressure, really, that got me into this. I was always taught as a boy in my family not to run away from anything. If you were convinced you ought to do it, try to do it."

The doubts he had about giving up the diplomatic service were shared by his family, who thought that though it would be fine for Dad to become foreign minister, it would also mean he would have to go into politics. The deciding factor in his mind, however, was the outlook if he did not accept St. Laurent's cabinet offer. The two of them were deeply involved, in the summer and fall of 1948, in the effort to organize NATO; the strong belief by St. Laurent in the collective-security principle was what made Pearson's work effective in promoting NATO despite Canada's past tradition of avoiding foreign commitments in peacetime. If St. Laurent, because of Pearson's refusal to join the cabinet, were to appoint someone else to the post, there was no telling who he would be and no assurance he would provide the same strong backing for Pearson, his chief diplomatic technician. For this reason Pearson decided it was his duty to make the change.

Once Pearson agreed, it was up to the Liberal party to get him elected to Parliament, since in Canada it is necessary for the governmental executive to hold a seat in the House— though it is also permissible occasionally to have a cabinet member from the Senate. The job of finding a "safe" Liberal constituency was turned over to Walter Harris, St. Laurent's minister of finance and big wheel in the party organization. Pearson declined a suggestion that he run from one of the Ottawa ridings. Ottawa's voters are overwhelmingly civil servants. Most were Liberal appointees, since Mackenzie King had been in power for twenty-five years with only two interruptions, one of them quite brief. Standing for the House of Commons from Ottawa seemed to Pearson less than sporting. Consequently, Harris arranged to make vacant the riding of Algoma East by the time-honored custom of promoting the incumbent, Thomas Farquhar, to the Senate. Pearson had never lived in the area, but that is not essential in Canada. Algoma East was, and is, a rural area east of Sault Ste Marie, bordering on Lake Huron's Georgian Bay, with much bush country but including the lovely forested and cultivated Manitoulin Island. It was Indian country, too, and it was not long before Pearson was acclaimed an honorary chief, in the accepted political tradition. With a clear majority over two opponents, Pearson comfortably won a by-election to succeed Farquhar.

Since that election he has been re-elected six times by the voters of Algoma East, with increasing majorities. Many of his constituents have become his good friends, and he has developed an attachment to the district that makes him look forward to his visits when he is able to get away from Ottawa.

One of his early trips as prime minister was to tour the constituency.

But though he now had to remember federal problems in towns such as Blind River, Little Current, Chapleau, Espanola, and Thessalon, in the sphere of diplomacy there was little to mark the transition except the air of added authority. As undersecretary and as minister, he was deeply involved in the flow of international events from 1946 to 1957, when the Liberals lost power.

Millions of words have been written and innumerable books published about those crisis-ridden years, though not in terms of Pearson's participation in them. To record all the diplomatic maneuvers in which he was involved, particularly during the year of 1952-53 when he was president of the General Assembly, would be a tedious recital except for specialized students of the era. Even as an organization without real authority, the United Nations bogs down in the legalisms, the national sensitivities, and the bureaucratic red tape of parliamentary institutions everywhere, to the point where the layman comes to despise the pettiness with which a fundamentally inspiring ideal is carried out in practice. The average reader gets lost trying to follow the distinctions between what the news accounts describe as "the nineteen-nation" resolution and the "seven-nation" proposal; nor does he find it of supreme importance to find out the difference between UNESCO and ECOSOC when he runs across accounts of the activities of the UN's specialized agencies. If he is a man of good will he accepts on faith all this effort on behalf of peace and a better world and is thankful someone else is paid to conduct it. But his interest soars in times of crisis, and of these the UN has had more than its share.

There were three crises, however, we might examine in connection with Pearson's career. They illustrate significantly the motivations that prompted his actions and that eventually won him a Nobel peace prize. The first was the Palestine crisis of 1947; the second the Korean war, which broke out in 1950; and the third was Suez, in 1956. In each, Canada need not have taken the initiatives she did; her delegation could have played a cautious role, looking for leadership from some larger power. But as a man taught not to run away from responsibility, Pearson thrust his country into active effort to solve the immediate problem and emerged with distinction. In each situation, also, there was a discernible pragmatism in the Canadian search for solution, a feeling for the practical method of damping down the flames of conflict, as distinct from the theoretical but impractical.

Pearson took command because as undersecretary, and later as foreign minister, he outranked the permanent representative of Canada to the United Nations whenever he attended its deliberations.

The Palestine crisis grew out of Great Britain's decision to end its mandate over a territory that had existed since the first world war. The United Nations called a special session of the General Assembly, which met from April 28 to May 15, 1947, to deal with the situation in view of the prospect that fighting would break out between the Jews and Arabs, as it did. The assembly set up a special committee on Palestine (promptly christened UNSCOP) that comprised eleven member countries, including Canada, which was represented by Justice Ivan C. Rand. UNSCOP visited Palestine in June and July. It came back divided over what to do, and submitted majority and minority reports when the assembly opened its regular

September session. Seven members, including Canada, favored partition of the area between Jews and Arabs, with economic union. Three recommended a federal state; the eleventh member wanted the whole problem turned back to the assembly. After setting up an *ad hoc* committee and going through a confused debate, the assembly adopted the principle of partition with economic union. On November 29 a resolution was introduced providing that Palestine be divided into an Arab state, a Jewish state, and the city of Jerusalem. The resolution called for freedom of transit between these areas and proposed that economic union be administered by a board of nine members.

Watching the reaction of the great powers and the interested parties, Canada noted that the U.S. favored the partition scheme; that Russia seemed to do the same, with different emphasis; that Great Britain sought only to release herself from the mandate; that the Jewish agency accepted the plan with some misgivings; and that the Arabs would have none of it.

Canada had no direct interest in Palestine, nor was the issue as much of a factor in domestic politics as in the U.S., but Pearson was seeking a solution that was assured of enough support to be workable. It was obvious that partition would be adopted by the assembly and also that the Arabs would resist it. No other solution, however, seemed to offer as much promise of avoiding conflict. Pearson argued that before any plan was adopted its method of application should be carefully defined. As a result the assembly set up a working group of four nations, on which Pearson represented Canada. With representatives of the U.S., Russia, and Guatemala, Pearson devised the partition scheme that eventually resulted in the creation of the state of Israel. Israel gave him its medallion of valor, and Pearson's underlings at the Department of External Affairs dubbed him "King of the Jews" behind his back.

Korea was equally remote from Canada's interest when the Communist invasion took place in June, 1950, except in terms of the collective-security principle of western defense that Canada had adopted. When the UN Security Council adopted a resolution urging a cease-fire and withdrawal of invading forces, and followed it by inviting its members to supply military units to repel the attack, Canada was prompt in responding. It made three destroyers available to the UN naval force, supplied air transport through Canadian Pacific Airlines, and —in a broadcast by St. Laurent—explained that while Canada was in no position to send over first-line elements of her army, she would contribute to any international force recruited by the Security Council. Recruitment of a special Canadian force of brigade strength for service in Korea was announced in August.

"This special force," Pearson told the House of Commons on August 31, "is unique in one way among the offers of military forces which have been made to the United Nations as the result of the war in Korea, and provides, I think, a valuable example and precedent. If other countries were, in the same way, to earmark a portion of their forces which might be made available to the UN for collective defense, there would be ready throughout the free world national contingents for a UN force which could be quickly brought together in the face of future emergency. In this way the UN would be equipped with that military strength which it was intended in the Charter it should have at its disposal but which, in fact, it never has had, largely because of the attitude of the U.S.S.R."

Ever since, Canada has maintained one brigade earmarked for possible call by the UN. It is the only UN member that has done this.

The United States, being most directly involved, was in the forefront of UN moves connected with the Korean conflict. Canada, however, became one of the seven sponsors of the assembly's "United for Peace" resolution that was brought forward to circumvent situations when the Security Council was paralyzed by veto. This resolution contained a recommendation that each UN member maintain special armed-force units for use as United Nations forces, and Pearson suggested that the UN study the idea of recruiting an international police force. One of the UN committees did go into the question, but found other noncommunist members unwilling to make physical contributions to such a body.

After the Chinese communists went massively to the aid of the North Koreans, Pearson's influence was exerted to put a brake on the MacArthur policy of carrying the war to the Chinese border. He opposed U.S. attempts to invoke sanctions against Peking. In a speech to the Canadian Bar Association on March 31, 1951, he agreed that the UN had to recognize unprovoked aggression and condemn it, but that this "should not mean that in every case economic and military sanctions must follow." Enforcement action, he contended, "must be related to the practicability of such action, to the general strategic and political situation . . . we should recognize our limitations in this way." He was fearful that imposition of sanctions would only spread the war to China instead of keeping it localized.

Nevertheless when the General Assembly requested its president, Nasrollah Entezam, to serve on a three-man committee to see whether a cease-fire could be arranged, Pearson accepted the draft to serve with him and India's Sir Benegal Rau. The committee, spurned in attempts to deal reasonably with Peking, brought in a report outlining the basic elements for settlement. Though the eventual truce took more than two years to bring about, it was accomplished along the lines of the Entezam-Pearson-Rau report. In the long deadlock over Peking's insistence on the return of all prisoners of war, Pearson played a significant behind-the-scenes role in reconciling the procedure proposed by India and the fears of the United States that such a procedure failed to safeguard the rights of prisoners.

His role in the Suez crisis was much more central and dramatic.

Pearson was in Ottawa on October 29, 1956, when he learned of the British-French-Israeli invasion of Egypt. In New York, at the United Nations Security Council, the United States introduced a resolution calling for a cease-fire and withdrawal of the invading troops. This resolution was vetoed by Britain and France, both of which were permanent members of the Council, and the U.S. promptly moved to carry the fight into the General Assembly, where the veto did not apply. The General Assembly was called into emergency session for Thursday, November 1. Pearson, after consultation with Prime Minister St. Laurent, flew to New York and arrived just as the organization was beginning its deliberations, at 9:50 P.M.

Canada was in a difficult position in view of the violent split between its three closest friends. Its first task was to decide how to vote on the U.S. resolution. Pearson would have liked more time, but the U.S. was pressing for decision and the assembly was in a mood for action. Pearson did not even get time to speak before the vote, which resulted in adoption of the resolution, 64 to 5. Canada was among six nations that abstained. Pearson did, however, get a chance to explain the abstention shortly afterward.

Canada favored parts of the resolution, he said, and deemed it to be "a moderate proposal couched in reasonable and objective terms, without unfair or unbalanced condemnation," and therefore could not bring itself to vote against it; at the same time Canada felt it was inadequate as it stood and that more time should have been allowed to improve it. "I confess to a feeling of sadness, indeed even distress, at not being able to support the position taken by two countries whose ties with my country are and will remain close and intimate," he said, "two countries which have contributed so much to man's progress and freedom under law; and two countries which are Canada's mother countries." He argued that as it stood, the assembly's recommendation as embodied in the resolution could not be effective without the compliance of the states to which it was directed. "I had ventured to hope," he said, "that by a short delay and in informal talks we might have made some headway in securing a favorable response before the vote was taken from those governments and delegations which will be responsible for carrying it out."

He conceded that a cease-fire and withdrawal of troops was of greatest urgency. "But," he added, "it does not provide for any steps to be taken by the United Nations for a peace settlement, without which a cease-fire will be of only temporary value at best." Suppose the troops did withdraw to the old Arab-Israeli armistice lines, he went on: what then?

"What then, six months from now? Are we to go through all this again? Are we to return to the status quo? Such a return would not be to a position of security, or even a tolerable position, but would be a return to terror, bloodshed, strife, incidents, charges and counter charges, and ultimately another explosion which the United Nations Truce Supervision Organization would be powerless to prevent and possibly even to investigate."

He said what he would have liked to see included in the resolution was some provision authorizing the secretary-general to make arrangements with member states "for a United Nations force large enough to keep these borders at peace while a political settlement is being worked out."

He continued: "I hope that even now, when action on the resolution has been completed, it may not be too late to give consideration to this matter. My own government would be glad to recommend Canadian participation in such a United Nations force, a truly international peace and police force."

The idea of an international police force, which had been talked of even before the United Nations came into being, persisted in Pearson's mind. Previous speakers during the debate on the Suez resolution had mentioned it. But it was Pearson's speech that attracted the attention of U.S. Secretary of State John Foster Dulles. Taking the floor toward the end of the session, which lasted until 4:20 A.M., Friday, November 2, Dulles said:

"In my opening remarks I spoke of the importance of a constructive and positive development of this situation, and not merely attempting to turn the clock back. Mr. Pearson, the representative of Canada, also spoke rather fully upon

that point, and I want to emphasize my complete agreement
with what he said, and not only my personal agreement, but
the feeling of President Eisenhower, with whom I talked a
few hours ago about this aspect of the matter. It is a phase of
the situation which we deem of the utmost importance, and
the United States delegation would be very happy indeed if
the Canadian delegation would formulate and introduce as
part of these proceedings a concrete suggestion along the lines
that Mr. Pearson outlined."

What attracted Dulles to the Canadian suggestion was that
it went beyond merely advancing an idea; it renewed Canada's specific offer to provide troops, as in the Korean crisis.
The U.S. endorsement opened an opportunity for Pearson
that he proceeded to exploit in what proved to be the most
dramatic highlight of his diplomatic career and led to his
being awarded the Nobel Peace Prize the following year.

The incident illustrated more clearly than any other in
which Pearson engaged how a middle power that is alert to
its opportunities can move in and provide leadership when
a clash among the great powers leaves international affairs
disorganized.

In the early days of the United Nations, "management"
of the rather loosely organized General Assembly was conducted by Great Britain. As the master of international diplomacy between the wars, staffed with an experienced and able
diplomatic service, the U.K. supplied behind-the-scenes guidance the United States was not yet as qualified to give and
that neither country would accept from Soviet Russia. Dag
Hammarskjold had strong ideas about the limitations of his
own position as far as taking the initiative, and he was in the
habit of taking counsel from Great Britain—not so much in

regard to the UN's policy direction as its organizational structure and the handling of its business. This "management" influence of the British had begun to break down after the UN expanded its membership in 1955 to take in a number of Asian and African states, but it still existed to a degree—until Suez. At that point, with the two mainstays of the West at loggerheads, the UN was left without any one state to look to for the taking of action.

What the Suez situation called for was a "floor manager" who would guide it toward specific action, and this is what Pearson became. He was able to step into the role partly because he had advanced a specific suggestion that had quickly been picked up and endorsed by the United States, but also because as an old UN hand and former president of the assembly he was on first-name terms with most of the delegates. Hardly anyone else had the same wide acquaintance, respect, and, at the same time, knowledge of assembly procedures and "feel" for its politics.

Pearson's first move was to fly back to Ottawa for conferences with St. Laurent and the cabinet. With St. Laurent's backing, he got cabinet approval to offer a specific resolution embodying the police-force idea. He was given blanket authority for the proposal and complete latitude to decide, on the basis of his judgment of the UN's temper, not only when to introduce a resolution but whether to introduce it at all.

Armed with this authority, Pearson flew back to New York for the second emergency session of the assembly, which had been set for Saturday night, November 3. On his arrival he conferred separately with the British and American permanent representatives, first with Sir Pierson Dixon and then with Henry Cabot Lodge, in a spare office of the secretariat

112

building. The move he outlined was a proposal requesting Hammarskjold to draw up plans for an emergency police force to supervise a cease-fire in accordance with the terms of the resolution already adopted. Both representatives approved, as did Dulles, who arrived a bit later. Pearson had to deal with the two delegations separately as they were scarcely on speaking terms. He told them both they would have to leave to him the judgment when and whether to go ahead. "I don't want to go off half-cocked," he told them, "and I don't want to take an initiative that is going to boomerang. You will just have to leave it to me to decide whether this is something that has to be done. I'll follow the debate and see what the feeling is."

Pearson then broached his proposal to Hammarskjold. He found the secretary-general very doubtful about its wisdom on the ground of timing and tactics. Hammarskjold seemed not to take the Egyptian crisis as seriously as did Pearson, suggesting that it would work itself out. Pearson felt it was rapidly deteriorating into what might become a serious conflict involving other states. An hour later, however, Hammarskjold returned to Pearson to inform him that on reflection he had concluded it was necessary to take action.

Debate in the plenary session started off on the basis of two U.S. resolutions, one proposing a committee of five countries to prepare recommendations for the settlement of the major problems outstanding between the Arabs and Israelis, the second proposing a three-nation group to take whatever steps were necessary to reopen the Suez Canal and operate it with freedom of passage to all. In hindsight, both were too far-reaching in the context of the moment, with fighting still going on. As debate went on, India came forward with a resolution on behalf of nineteen nations, designed to put the UN on record with a second demand for cease-fire and withdrawal. As the fighting in Egypt had only intensified after the UN's first vote on the subject, there seemed scant hope that a repetition of the request would be any more effective. Judging the time ripe for some move that would facilitate compliance with the original resolution, Pearson offered Canada's resolution. It requested that the secretary-general submit to the assembly within forty-eight hours, "a plan for the setting up, with the consent of the nations concerned, of an emergency international United Nations force to secure and supervise the cessation of hostilities" in accordance with the terms of the November 2 resolution.

"The immediate purpose of our meeting tonight is to bring about as soon as possible a cease-fire and a withdrawal of forces, in the area which we are considering, from contact and from conflict with each other," Pearson told the assembly. "Our longer range purpose, which has already been referred to tonight and which may ultimately, in its implications, be even more important, is to find solutions for the problems which, because we have left them unsolved over the years, have finally exploded into this fighting and conflict."

With some polite words for the "longer range purpose" of the U.S. resolutions, he turned to the Indian proposal and questioned whether its provisions for "making arrangements" with the warring parties for a cease-fire was "adequate machinery for this complicated and difficult task." He stressed that he was not opposing the Indian resolution, but he thought something more was needed.

"I do suggest," he said, "that the Secretary-General be given another and supplementary—not conflicting, but supplemen-

114

tary—responsibility: to work out at once a plan for an international force to bring about and supervise the cease-fire visualized in the Assembly resolution which has already been passed."

Lodge was quick to back him up on behalf of the U.S. "I want to say that the United States likes the Canadian draft resolution very much," said Lodge. "We are looking for something that will meet the immediate crisis which is in front of us, as well as something that will go to the causes and into the more long-range subjects." He said the U.S. would not press its resolutions to a vote. "We do think that the draft resolution submitted by the Canadian Secretary of State for External Affairs is one that should be acted on promptly, and we would like to see it given priority. We should like to see it acted on quickly this evening, because it contains a real hope of meeting the very grave emergency that confronts the world."

Subsequent debate raised two points of interpretation, which Pearson answered, and also revealed general support for the Canadian proposal. When the vote was put, the proposal was approved 57 to 0, with nineteen abstentions including the Soviet bloc and the combatant nations. It was another long night for the General Assembly, which remained in session until 3 A.M. Sunday.

Pearson in later years described the incident as the most dramatic forty-eight hours he ever spent in diplomacy, but also a disappointment in that it was never developed into achieving a political settlement of the longer range Arab-Israeli dispute. His two days in the world spotlight were only the beginning of weeks of intense effort to bring this about, but as the United Nations Emergency Force succeeded in its immediate task, the fear of wider conflict subsided and the crisis psychology needed to get things done disappeared.

Like all successful operations, the creation of UNEF seems relatively simple and logical in hindsight. The diplomatic skill it required becomes apparent only when one considers the numerous pitfalls Pearson avoided. It was painful, first of all, for a Canadian foreign minister to be forced to choose between the United States and Great Britain over an issue so important and fundamental. In his own country there were some who were inclined to crow over the mess the British had got into; others were angry over U.S. interference and passionately in favor of supporting Britain. Some French Canadians were sympathetic to France, which was in the UN doghouse. Pearson had to sell his own cabinet on a course of action in the face of these domestic attitudes and then pick his way through the trackless UN to carry it out.

One of the officials who was advising Pearson at the time described some of the diplomatic footwork that went into it: "The British and French said they wanted to interpose themselves between Egypt and Israel, but they had no legal right to do it. The best way to bail them out and still prevent a blowup was to have the UN take over.

"One way to do it was to turn the British-French forces into a UN force, but that was not possible because of strong UN feeling against the two nations. Mike had always been interested in the idea of an international force. It would be foolish to say it was a unique Canadian idea, but we had been thinking along those lines, and so had the U.S. Someone had to take the initiative. The whole Assembly wanted something done, even the British and the French. It was necessary to get the maximum support. Dulles knew that if the U.S. proposed

116

it, it would become a cold-war issue. Mike was able to do it because he was well thought of by the Israelis, he had been President of the Assembly, he knew half of the Foreign Ministers by their first names, he had the support of the U.S., and the Egyptian Minister, Fawzi, could talk to him rationally.

"He had to play a double game. To get the Arabs and Asians to support it he had to make it seem that the UN was 'driving out' the British and French. At the same time he had to give the British and French a satisfactory reason for backing out: the reason that the UN was 'taking over.' It was a ticklish business. Egypt at first said no, but Fawzi understood his problem and was able to talk Nasser into being sensible."

Another Canadian, Major General E. L. M. Burns, chief of staff of the UN Truce Supervision Organization, worked closely with Pearson and Secretary-General Hammarskjold in working out the technical problems of actually bringing a military force into being. Acting on Hammarskjold's report, on November 7 the assembly approved recruiting such a peace army from nations not represented on the permanent membership of the Security Council. In the end Canada's contribution was almost entirely comprised of headquarters personnel rather than fighting troops. Only two days later advance units of the force began assembling at a staging area near Naples, and on November 15 the first units reached the Suez Canal Zone.

There was a lot more work to be done and more UN resolutions to pass in subsequent weeks and months, in connection with clearing the canal of sunken ships to permit resumption of navigation and persuading Israel to withdraw from the Sinai Peninsula. Pearson was active on Canada's behalf in all of it, but by that time the direction of UN policy was fixed and it carried on under its own momentum until, the danger past, it petered out. The novel demonstration of how a peace force could be made to work was left as an example without inspiring the nations to build it into an instrument of more general application. It should be noted in passing that Pearson's effort was motivated primarily by a positive desire to promote international peace. He was not prompted by any particularly Canadian national interest except that of seeking to overcome a split between Canada's closest friends. It was another effort Pearson made in the spirit of "waging" the peace.

Back in Ottawa, St. Laurent called a special session of Parliament to authorize the Canadian contribution to the UNEF. Although acclaimed widely by his fellow diplomats in other countries, Pearson for the first time came under heavy attack by his domestic opposition. Two strong critics were the acting Conservative opposition leader, W. Earl Rowe, and a man who was to occupy Pearson's portfolio a few years later, Howard Green.

"Let not the government believe it can any longer deceive the Canadian people by creating a fancy halo around the Secretary of State for External Affairs, as if he had already saved the world's peace and solved the Suez Canal crisis," said Rowe. Green described Pearson as having made Canada a "chore boy for the United States," and added: "It is high time Canada had a government which will not knife Canada's best friends in the back."

Pearson defended himself vigorously. He said Canada was deeply mindful of the need, throughout the crisis, of holding the British Commonwealth together. "At one stage after the fighting on land began it was on the verge of dissolution, and that is not an exaggerated observation," he said. He did not elaborate the reference, but those aware of the attitude of India's Krishna Menon knew what he meant. Pearson said it was "nonsensical chatter" to criticize Canada either as having acted as an American stooge or as having "lined up with the Russians."

"We thought," he said, "it was the right action for a Canadian delegation to take. It was an objective attitude, it was a Canadian attitude, and it was an independent attitude."

Pearson learned from the press that he had won the Nobel peace prize. It was on the day Prime Minister John Diefenbaker was facing his first parliament, in October, 1957. Pearson was in his first-floor office in the center block of the parliament buildings, reflecting gloomily that it was Mr. St. Laurent and he who had originally invited the queen to come to Ottawa for the ceremony of opening, which is usually performed by her representative in Canada, the governor general. Now, as a result of the 1957 election, another government was in charge.

The telephone rang. It was a call from Canadian Press.

"What comment do you have on winning the Nobel peace prize?" the reporter asked.

"What!" Pearson exploded. "You must be mistaken. It must be that I have been nominated for the prize. I've been nominated before."

"Just a minute, I'll check," said the reporter. "No, that's right, you've been awarded the prize."

"Gosh!" said Pearson. "I'll have to call my wife and let her know."

That night, at the state dinner at Rideau Hall, the queen

took him aside for a few moments to compliment him on the honor and on being the first Canadian to win it.

The cash involved in the prize gave Pearson his first sense of financial security. Had he died before he won that award, Mrs. Pearson would have had to go to work to support herself. He bought bonds with the prize money and ever since has devoted the interest on them to a private charity. By the time he became prime minister he had accumulated pension rights and other savings that left him more secure.

9

Conviviality Beyond the Call of Duty

WHILE HE was foreign minister, Pearson was given a unique opportunity to study Russia and her leaders close up on a tour of the Soviet Union.

It began in 1955 with an incident at the San Francisco meeting at which the United Nations celebrated the tenth anniversary of its founding, in the same city where it had started life. In a street back of the Opera House, Soviet Foreign Minister Vyacheslav M. Molotov buttonholed his Canadian counterpart and invited him to visit the Soviet Union.

It was quite a surprising invitation and created a bit of a sensation later on when Pearson announced he had accepted. He was the first of the NATO ministers to visit Russia. In 1955 the West had been plunged into one of its periodic fits of suspicion and depression about communist intentions by the discovery that Moscow had entered into a deal with Abdul Gamal Nasser to supply Egypt with arms. This threatened to upset the uneasy balance of power that had existed in the Middle East between Israel and the Arab states since the Palestine truce.

Pearson felt that a "good will" trip was not sufficient justification for visiting the Soviet Union and that the trip ought to have some other purpose. Indications from the Russians had led Canada to believe that Moscow would welcome a trade agreement. The type in vogue at the time was the "most favored nation" treaty under which a country would agree to offer some other nation the same break on tariff concessions as she gave her most favored trading partner. But such a treaty was of little value to Russia, and after some study it was decided something more tangible was called for. The decision was to offer Moscow a contract to buy Canadian wheat. Pearson decided to take along the deputy minister of trade and commerce, Mitchell Sharp, to conduct the negotiations.

Before the tour began, a completely unrelated by-product resulted from consultations over the arrangements. Pearson asked Paul Martin, who was then heading the Canadian delegation to the United Nations, to call on Molotov to discuss the travel plans and while he was there to ask him if something could not be done about a deadlock in the UN over membership. Nearly a score of new nations had come into being since the UN had last increased its membership, and Russia was blocking their admission because the United States objected to membership for Outer Mongolia. The U.S. was questioning whether Outer Mongolia, that buffer area between China and Russia, was in truth an independent nation comparable to those which had been granted full freedom from various colonial powers. Martin told the Russian that Pearson believed the United Nations should be a "universal" body, and asked whether something could be done to break the deadlock.

To Martin's utter surprise, Molotov replied: "This is a good time." It was characteristic of the Russians to make unexpected moves without apparent motivation, and Martin figured it was just plain luck that he broached the idea at a time when the Russians were ready to act. Martin got credit for the subsequent "package deal" that admitted sixteen new nations to the international body, but he said "It was Mike's idea."

Pearson took off for Moscow at the end of September, 1955. When he landed in London on October 1 he found Prime Minister Anthony Eden worried about the violent reaction in Washington to the Soviet-Egyptian arms deal. He was thinking of making a personal appeal to Soviet Prime Minister Nikolai Bulganin not to start an arms race between the Arab countries and Israel. He showed Pearson the draft of a letter he wanted the Americans to support and suggested that Pearson might back it up in any talks he had with Bulganin or Khrushchev. Pearson said he might be willing, but only if the U.S. supported Eden's initiative. As it turned out, however, this subject did not come up during the trip.

Five days later the Canadian party flew into Moscow in the Royal Canadian Air Force's C-5, a unique, long-range airplane created by adding a middle section to a DC-4, pressurizing it, and installing more powerful motors. In addition to Pearson and Mitchell Sharp, the party included John Holmes, George Ignatiev, and Ray Crepault of the Department of External Affairs. Ignatiev was of Russian extraction.

The Russians rolled out the red carpet for the visitors. The first night's entertainment was a ballet, *Don Quixote*, at the Bolshoi Theatre. Molotov and Zorin ushered them into what once was the royal box of the famous theater, and a spotlight played on them while the crowd gave them a standing ovation. "It makes me feel like the Czar," Mike whispered to one of his companions when the lights went down. "The Little Elgin was never like this." (The Little Elgin is an Ottawa movie theater.) Pearson discovered the ballet lived up to the Bolshoi's reputation of being just about perfect.

Next day he had his first meeting with Molotov. He found the Russian minister cautious and noncommittal as he discussed international affairs, with Oleg Troyanovsky interpreting. Molotov listened to Pearson's ideas on the future of Germany, on disarmament, and on the danger of forcing "domestic" questions into the agenda of the United Nations. Vaguely he talked of the possibility that elections might be held in Vietnam with some help from the international control commission, of which Canada was a member. He refused to be drawn out on the situation in Laos, but was interested in Pearson's views on Korea and China.

Though he felt he had to be equally cautious and noncommittal, Pearson did let Molotov know that Canada did not agree with all points of United States policy on China, particularly with respect to the offshore islands. Canada, he said, was taking a new look at Peking; Canadian public opinion was moving toward appreciation of the facts of the situation, but many in North America regarded Communist China as a dangerous threat to the peace. Canada did not intend to get into any unnecessary difficulties with the U.S. on this item of policy.

At a luncheon following the conference, Pearson sat next to Georgi Malenkov, found him witty, intelligent, and interesting but judged that his survival value was not as high as Molotov's.

Next morning Pearson initiated the trade talks Mitchell Sharp was to carry on. The Russians kept asking embarrassing questions about the "strategic list" of goods that Canada, as a NATO member, was pledged not to ship to communist countries. Pearson referred to the "list of shortages," but he knew he wasn't fooling the Soviets. "These chaps don't allow their friendly toasting off-duty to interfere with tough negotiation, nor must we," he commented to one of his aides.

After that session Pearson left the negotiating job to Sharp and set off by train to Leningrad on a sightseeing trip as the guest of the government. Comparing notes with the rest of his party at the day's end, he was surprised to find that Russians generally, while always friendly, were very frank, quite willing to broach controversial subjects, and seemed really to believe that the U.S. had aggressive designs on Russia. This fear of America, he concluded, was not confined to high political figures but to artists and scientists and technicians as well. He could not help wondering to what extent the top political officials were fomenting the fear for their own purposes.

"Incidentally," Pearson remarked to one of his staff after the Leningrad stop, "nobody ever seems to mention Stalin. Lenin and Marx, yes; Stalin, no. Is he being allowed to slide back into history as an ordinary personage instead of a communist god?" It was almost a year before news of Khrushchev's denunciation of Stalin leaked out of Russia, but the downgrading had already begun in the minds of Stalin's successors and Pearson sensed it.

From Leningrad Pearson returned to Moscow to see how

the trade negotiations were getting along (there was a long hassle over eliminating communist propaganda from the communiqué) and to return his hosts' hospitality by entertaining at a luncheon at the Canadian Embassy.

In his toast at that affair Pearson mentioned that geography had placed Canada strategically between the United States and the Soviet Union, making it subject to pressures from both sides, though of very different kinds. Lazar Kaganovich, the top trade negotiator for the Russians and ranking guest at the luncheon, commented in his response that as far as the U.S.S.R. was concerned, the pressure on Canada was friendly pressure.

"The strongest pressure in the world can be friendly pressure," Pearson reminded him.

The luncheon also served to celebrate the success of the negotiations, which led to a firm order from the Soviets for 400,000 tons of wheat a year for three years. Then Pearson was ready to fly to the Crimea for a visit with Khrushchev, who was vacationing. For this leg the Russians supplied a plane of their own, a plushly appointed DC-3 *Dakota*. Pearson was accompanied by John Watkins, Canadian ambassador in Moscow; Ray Crepault; and George Ignatiev. The Russians included Troyanovsky, who was to interpret, and the MVD guards who had been assigned to the party.

In 1955 the Russians were still maintaining great secrecy about Khrushchev's vacation hideaway. It was only later that visiting Khrushchev either at the Kremlin or in Crimea became a regular trip for world statesmen. Pearson did not know when he left Moscow just what his destination was, though he had reason to believe it was Yalta, which proved correct. Landing at Sevastopol, a naval base ordinarily out of bounds to foreign officials and visitors, the party started off across the field on which the famed Light Brigade had fought at Balaclava. They reached a mountainous coast where the road snaked over hairpin turns with sheer drops of hundreds of feet. Their destination turned out to be an elaborate mansion right on the sea, situated amid lush gardens and rocky patches. "Proletarian luxury de luxe," Pearson remarked when he saw it. He was met at the door by a lady doctor who had heard that in Moscow he had picked up a bad cold and laryngitic throat, and who insisted on giving him some pills and a gargle solution. The treatment, he noticed, helped his voice return to normal during the afternoon.

At 8 P.M. the four Canadians were driven from their guest house to the fabulous Yusupof Palace where Khrushchev and Bulganin were scheduled to entertain them at dinner. The two Russian leaders met them at the door: Khrushchev with his look of a Ukrainian peasant, Bulganin well dressed and courtly in manner. Pearson later remarked to one of his party that while Bulganin had the look of a man at home in a palace that had once belonged to a favorite of the Czar, there was no mistaking that it was Khrushchev who acted as if he felt at home.

Khrushchev lived up to his reputation for frankness by opening the conversation immediately with a blunt attack on NATO as a threat to the Soviet Union. Pearson took exception, saying one reason he had lost his voice in Moscow was that he had talked so much about the purely defensive character of NATO as well as of United States foreign policy. It was absurd, he said, to think that the United States or any other western government wanted war. The party moved to a conference room and talked for a couple of hours before dinner. When Khrushchev suggested they eat, the Canadians followed him down the hall to a great dining room where a table was spread with every kind of Russian food and drink— Khrushchev taking occasion on the way to point out the location of three bathrooms—and after they sat down he asked his guests if they would mind if his family joined the group. "They are hungry too," he said. He left the room and returned with Mrs. Khrushchev, explaining that his daughter had grown tired of waiting and had gone to the movies.

Khrushchev indicated intense interest in George Ignatiev. He obviously had been briefed on his background. He kept referring to him as "the Count" in a way that seemed to waver between disdain and respect. Khrushchev and Bulganin proposed toast after toast in the Russian style. "Drink up like a Russian," Khrushchev kept telling Ignatiev.

Bulganin proposed one toast to Prime Minister St. Laurent, commenting that he knew Pearson was on very close and friendly terms with him. With that as a cue, he emphasized that he and Nikita were on the same intimate terms, having worked together as the closest of friends for years, and that they would continue to do so in concert with their colleagues. This was not the first time during the trip it had been strongly hinted to Pearson that post-Stalin Russia was being ruled by a "collective" government. That, of course, was the theme of Khrushchev's denunciation of Stalin the following year—the days of the "cult of personality" and one-man rule were over. Later, in discussing the dinner with his party, Pearson said that while this might be true for the time being, he wondered how long the "group" government would last as such.

Another toast was to President Eisenhower's recovery, and

that led both Khrushchev and Bulganin to say, with what seemed genuine respect, how much they had been impressed by Eisenhower at the Geneva summit conference the previous summer. Khrushchev went even further, remarking that he even had established good personal relations with John Foster Dulles, surprised to find that Dulles was a man he could talk to. But Americans generally, complained Khrushchev, talked too much, boasted too much, and had no realization what war and sacrifice and fighting meant—and that was the great danger.

Pearson contradicted this. He added that Canadians knew what war meant. Twice, he noted, Canada had gone to war and suffered greatly in casualties even though she had not been directly attacked and even though she was remote from the actual conflict. Khrushchev accepted this, saying the Canadians were a fine fighting race and he hoped there would never be a war between Canada and the Soviet Union. During the evening he had a good deal to say about war and the might of Russian arms, but each time he always added: "However, there need not be any war if NATO doesn't attack, because we will never attack anybody."

It was after midnight before the Canadians managed to take leave of Khrushchev and return to their mansion. In a subsequent report on the evening's talk they took occasion to hope that Ottawa appreciated their effort at "conviviality beyond the line of duty." None of the four felt very bright next day when they were driven back to the airfield over the same hairpin roads. When one of the Russian escorts pointed out a monument erected where Marshal Kutusof (an ancestor of Ignatiev's), had lost an eye defeating the Turks, Pearson's groaning reply was: "You might raise a monument to me back at that place where I lost my stomach."

From Sevastopol they flew to Saky, where the Canadian *C-5* had brought the rest of the Pearson party. From there they flew out of Soviet territory, over Turkey, and down the Euphrates to Basra in Iraq, on their way to a meeting in India.

10

Leader of the Opposition

EVERY SO OFTEN a democratic nation seems destined to surprise itself with the results of an election. For the United States the surprise came in 1948, when Harry S. Truman won an upset victory over Thomas E. Dewey. The pollsters had it going the other way; no one, it seemed, gave Truman a chance except Truman himself and a few close friends. Afterward there were plenty who claimed they had guessed right all along, but they were not in evidence before the votes were counted.

For Canada the surprise came in 1957. John Diefenbaker, who had been chosen leader of the Progressive Conservatives less than a year before, headed a ticket that upset all calculations by winning seven more seats than the veteran Liberal prime minister, Louis St. Laurent. His victory brought to an abrupt end twenty-two years of uninterrupted Liberal rule.

On the testimony of one of Diefenbaker's campaign work-ers of that year, the Tory leader was as surprised as anyone. The aide recalls that it was only as the Diefenbaker party was flying on election night from Prince Albert to Regina, Saskatchewan, in order to be within reach of television when it became necessary to make a statement, that returns coming in over the plane radio convinced them that a Conservative victory was in the making. The realization suddenly hit home that Diefenbaker faced the task of putting together a government.

The Liberals, understandably, were stunned. They had expected their existing majority would be reduced, but not that they would lose power. This was also the popular expectation in advance of the voting, just as in the United States the public that voted for Truman had not really expected that he could make it on his own after succeeding to the presidency after Franklin Roosevelt's death. The confident expectation in Canada had been that St. Laurent, who was seventy-five, would carry the party through the 1957 election and then step down to give a younger man the leadership and the post of prime minister.

Two Liberal cabinet ministers were in the running for the succession. Walter Harris, whose portfolio was finance, had the support of the party organizations. Paul Martin, who administered health and welfare, was a contender chiefly on the basis of ambition for the job; he was an experienced politician, a good speaker, and a man of ingratiating personality. But Martin, of French stock and a Catholic from Windsor, Ontario, had the handicap of seeking to succeed a French Catholic. The Liberals, who had been headed by only three leaders in the history of their party, had established a tradition of rotating the office. Sir Wilfred Laurier, the first, was French Catholic; William Lyon Mackenzie King, the second, was English Protestant; Louis St. Laurent, the third, was French Catholic. Now it was the turn of an English-speaking Protestant, which meant front-runner Harris. There was little mention of anyone but Harris and Martin, and none at all of Pearson.

But the election rudely changed all that. The antigovernment swing cut down such a prominent Liberal as C. D. Howe and eight other cabinet ministers, including Harris, who had gone down to defeat in Ontario's Grey-Bruce riding before a Progressive Conservative, Eric Winkler.

Despite the rude shock of losing power, many Liberal leaders looked on the result as no more than a temporary setback. After all, Diefenbaker was in a minority position, even though he had more seats than the Liberals. A minority government always faced pitfalls in the House of Commons; even if it survived, there would always be another election when the party would regain what it had come to regard as its right to rule. Those who reasoned in this fashion were only demonstrating the truth of what a great Canadian editor, the late John W. Dafoe of the *Winnipeg Free Press,* had written years before. In a trenchant commentary issued under the title *Laurier, a Study in Canadian Politics,* Dafoe philosophized about the Laurier era, of which he was a part, and revealed great insight into human nature and the nature of politics.

"Parties, in reality, are organized states within the state," Dafoe wrote. "They have their own dynasties and hierarchies; and their reason for existence is to clothe themselves with the powers, functions, and glory of the state which they control.

133

Their desire is for absolute and continuing control to which they come to think they have a prescriptive right; and they never leave office without a sense of outrage. There never yet was a party ejected from office which did not feel pretty much as the Stuarts did when they lost the throne of England; the incoming administration is invariably regarded by them in the light of usurpers."

Thus did the Liberals of 1957 look upon the upstart Conservatives; thus did Diefenbaker look on the Pearson victory of 1963. In both cases the politicians were too close to events to recognize the detached truth in Dafoe's observation that "the people by a sure instinct compel a change in administration every now and then; but they move so slowly that a government well entrenched in office can usually outstay its welcome by one term of office."

Not all Liberals, however, looked on the election results as indicating only a temporary aberration on the part of the Canadian people. Some saw much more clearly that the Liberal party as it then existed, crusted with aged leadership and grown gouty with the perquisites of power to which it had become accustomed, had been completely repudiated by the voters. The comparative closeness of the vote was not a true measure of the extent to which Canadians had become disenchanted with their rulers. Political analysts could see, later on, how that fact was obscured by regional factors. At the time it was difficult to plumb the silent but deep protest by the voters. What Dafoe had described as the "sure instinct" of the people was at work.

One Liberal who sensed the voters' mood more clearly was a young man lately from England who had emigrated to Canada in 1954 to become editor of the *Winnipeg Free Press*.

He was Tom Kent, a tall, thin figure of somewhat saturnine countenance who looked like someone out of an El Greco portrait.

Kent had gotten to know Pearson during the Suez crisis. The *Free Press,* and Kent, did not approve Britain's attempt to settle its quarrel with Nasser by force of arms, and Kent discovered that the conclusions he reached in writing editorials for his newspaper closely paralleled the attitudes expressed by the minister for external affairs. Pearson, on his part, was pleased that a recently transplanted Englishman, thinking independently, had come to what he considered a North American view, as distinct from a British view, of the crisis. This led to the development of a friendly association between them, as the *Free Press* editor made occasional trips to Ottawa to explore the thinking of government leaders.

Two or three days after the party's 1957 defeat, Kent called on Pearson in his East Block office and found him cleaning out his papers to make way for his successor. Pearson was interested in Kent's ideas as to the reasons for the defeat. Pearson agreed with Kent's feeling, shared by many others, that the party had lost touch with the people after years in power, and also with Kent's view that as a factor in Canadian national politics the Liberals had been destroyed more completely than the narrowness of defeat revealed. The young editor argued that any party with the wit and timing to exploit the Liberals' demoralization could take over from them as the main opposition to the Conservatives, and that the only way in which the Liberals could re-establish themselves as one of the two major parties was by rebuilding from the roots up. Furthermore, he said, it would take more than one election to do it.

Pearson remarked, "Well, the election has certainly settled one thing for me. With so many of our ministers defeated, I'll have to stay here and work to rebuild the party."

Kent was among a number of Pearson's friends who argued that of those available for the leader's job, only Pearson combined the experience, the public stature, the devotion to Liberal principles, and the leadership attraction required to perform the task. Pearson agreed that if he felt duty-bound to work for the restoration of the Liberals as a national force, it followed that he had to accept requests of his friends to become a candidate for the leadership. The same call of duty applied to both steps toward the goal he accepted. Kent was impressed with the unemotional way in which the man who did not take easily to politics reached a reasoned conclusion about his duty and even accepted the proposition that he would have to go through at least one defeat. Kent told him that though he believed in a newspaperman's duty to think independently—as the *Free Press* had demonstrated in its criticism of Liberal ministers when it felt they were straying from liberal doctrine—he wanted to help Pearson in any way he could toward achievement of what they both sought.

Pearson thanked him for the offer. It was several months before he made use of it. In the meantime he had doubts about his decision and talked often about it with his close friend Walter Gordon, with Grant Dexter, a Winnipeg newspaperman assigned to Ottawa, and with others.

Unknown to Kent or to Pearson as they talked these things over in Ottawa, a group of young Liberals had just held a post-mortem on the election in Toronto's King Edward Hotel, the day after the vote. They were young men who had taken part in the campaign and who were as surprised as anyone

136

by the outcome. Their meeting was not by design, for no one had sent out a call; it was as if they could not deflate from their campaign activity overnight, and independently they drifted into campaign headquarters on the "morning after" to talk and figure out what had happened. They were in no sense an organized segment of the party, for they had only two things in common: their youth—none was over 35—and their admiration for Mike Pearson.

Pearson had, in fact, been an uncommonly attractive figure to Canada's young intellectuals ever since he first began to achieve prominence as a career diplomat. It was Pearson for whom Young Liberal groups most frequently asked when they sent to headquarters to get a speaker for their conventions and rallies.

The pull from intellectuals to get him into politics had been evident as early as 1945. The writer Ralph Allen, interviewing Pearson after he was made chairman of the United Nations' Food and Agriculture Organization, remarked: "Pearson would be a prize catch for anyone's party." He queried Pearson about political ambition and quoted him as replying: "This (diplomacy) is my job. You have to live in a constituency if you are going to get anywhere in Canadian politics. You have to own a business there, or have a job. And unless you have financial resources, you can't get anywhere." Three years later, shortly before Pearson made the break from diplomacy to politics, correspondent John Bird, writing in the *Ottawa Citizen,* mentioned him as potentially a good leader to succeed Mackenzie King, whose retirement was looming. But Bird dismissed the thought, saying "he has no party politics."

As for the group of about twenty-five young men who

met in the King Edward Hotel on what they remember as an extremely hot June day in 1957, Pearson had long been their idol. In retrospect, the group never had a name, even for identity; and they were not consciously a "Young Turk" organization, but as Liberals they had been doing independent thinking about the party succession and their thinking ran along the same lines. When St. Laurent stepped down they wanted Mike Pearson to be leader. The group included Keith Davey, who later become national organizer for two Pearson election bids.

These young men had, before the election, accepted as inevitable that Walter Harris would be the new leader. They wanted Mike Pearson, but they were not part of the "organization" and they assumed the politicians would prevail. Now Harris was gone because of his defeat, and in their minds Martin was Pearson's only obstacle. Their talk, however, was less about personalities than about the need to reform the party. The only way to reform the party, they decided, was to take over control, and that was what they set out to do. Informally they decided the initial step had to be achieving control of the national party's Ontario provincial organization. To this end they appointed Gordon Dryden, a young lawyer, as their chairman. Subsequently they placed members in party posts. Their activity was a long time in paying off, for the 1958 election intervened before their reform movement had a chance to take hold, but by the time of the 1962 election their steady work helped the Liberals win forty-four federal seats out of the eighty-five in Ontario, and this was an important element in the Liberal climb back to power, providing a momentum and "upswing" psychology that in 1963 enabled Ontario Liberals to sweep seventeen of Toron-

138

to's eighteen seats and win a total of fifty-two in the province.

But this all came later. In 1957, even though Pearson had come to the decision it was his duty to stand for the leadership if asked, it was unseemly for any candidate to indicate interest in the job until St. Laurent had made his own plans clear.

There was an incident connected with St. Laurent's announcement in August of his intention to retire that has never been detailed before. Pearson was attending a meeting of Ontario Young Liberals when he got a call from a member of the former prime minister's family asking him if he would pay a visit to St. Laurent. The caller said the Liberal leader was in poor health, very depressed, and anxious to retire but loath to do so lest the party feel that he was running away after a defeat. Pearson was told this fear of "letting the party down" was greatly worrying Mr. St. Laurent, and he was asked to see if he could reassure his elderly chief.

Pearson agreed, but asked that the visit be kept completely confidential. The Ontario Young Liberals had come out for younger leadership, and he did not want it assumed that his visit was as an emissary from them to persuade St. Laurent to resign. Also, he wanted someone else from the party to accompany him, so that it would not appear to be a personal effort on his part to replace St. Laurent. It was agreed that Lionel Chevrier, another onetime Liberal cabinet member, would go with him.

The two of them spent a day and a half with St. Laurent at St. Patrick, Quebec, where he was spending the summer. They convinced him that in view of the circumstances he would not be regarded as deserting the party if he wished to give up the leadership. As a result, a leadership convention was called for January, 1958, in Ottawa.

Martin, an indefatigable politician, familiar with all the tricks of the trade, began a quiet campaign in his own behalf. There was not much public activity, and none at all in behalf of Pearson. In October, Pearson won the Nobel Peace Prize, an event that gave him an enormous boost in prestige as the first Canadian selected for this great distinction, but he was still silent about his plans. Finally, on December 10, he said publicly that if the party wanted him he would accept the leadership.

As Martin's quiet campaign began to be felt in Toronto, the young Mike Pearson fans began to worry that the Windsor attorney would get the post by default, since Pearson apparently had no organization at work. Typical of the situation at the time was a telephone call from Martin to Keith Davey, one of the King Edward Hotel "reformers." Always a superb practitioner of the art of political blandishment, Martin had acquainted himself with the information that Davey had attended Victoria College, Pearson's school, and that Mrs. Davey was about to have a baby. Martin himself had studied at St. Michael's, another University of Toronto college. First Martin wanted to know, "how's that new baby?" Then he made his pitch: "Now Keith, we don't want to make this leadership contest a fight between Victoria and St. Michael's, do we?"

Davey, who was a bit surprised to receive such attention from a party big shot whom he did not know personally, worried that Martin's personal campaign would sew up the convention delegates before Mike got moving. He knew Walter Gordon only by reputation as Pearson's close friend. One Sunday morning he called up Gordon, introducing himself over the phone, and explaining his worry about Martin's activities. Gordon seemed unperturbed. He was not unappreciative, but all he could suggest was that Davey "talk it up" among admirers of Pearson. As the January convention date came closer, Davey called Gordon a second time to spread the alarm about Martin's campaign. This time Gordon was sufficiently impressed to invite Davey to show up at Ottawa the day before the meeting to see what could be done.

Davey's fears were somewhat allayed by the fact that the Young Liberals had sold the entire Toronto delegation on Mike. But he still worried about the rest of the country, for when they detrained in Ottawa, there on the steps of the Chateau Laurier, greeting the incoming delegates, was Paul Martin, shaking their hands and asking for their votes. Upstairs in Pearson's suite all was confusion. Nobody had any assigned task, and everyone was trying to do everything.

Pearson's amateur supporters knew that within the party as a whole there were many prominent figures who did not favor his candidacy. The hierarchy included a number of old-guard cabinet ministers and former ministers who still carried great weight in party councils and who were dubious about Pearson as the right man to lead an organization that would have to fight hard to regain power. Many senior Liberals looked on Pearson as a "do-gooder" type; a darling of the eggheads; a man who didn't understand what back-room politics was all about; a man, in fact, who even had an active distaste for all the cornball practices required in democracies for the winning of political power. The discouraging feature for the amateurs was that there was more than a little substance to this view. In one of his personal papers Pearson had put down as his formula for life: "to deserve success is more important than to achieve it." It was in keeping with

141

the creed learned from his father that his job was to improve the world in which he lived. At no time during his career had he really been exposed to the kind of political storms that inevitably beat around the head of a major party. His early career was in the academic field. As a diplomat he had been removed from politics. Even as cabinet minister he had escaped the partisan sniping his colleagues underwent, except in a few cases, such as the Suez incident. It was also true that while he did not shrink from the responsibilities that came his way, he did have a strong personal dislike for the wheeling and dealing of practical politics.

These misgivings about his chances proved groundless, however, once the vote was taken. On the first ballot Pearson got 1,074 votes to 305 for Martin, who moved immediately to make it unanimous.

With his acceptance speech, Pearson got a tremendously enthusiastic reception from his highly partisan audience. On behalf of the party he outlined an eight-point program that called for a "free and independent Canadianism, not narrow nationalism," promised "useful work for all Canadians who can work, and help for those who cannot," pledged continuous quest for social security, trade expansion with all nations, the sharing of wealth and the creation of new opportunities, the equalization of tax revenues to benefit the provinces and municipalities, and reiterated support for the Commonwealth, NATO, and the United Nations.

It was a speech well suited to the temper of the Liberal partisans who had selected him, but not to that of the Canadian people, who heard and saw it by television. An electorate that was still looking with hope at a new government was not in a mood to respond to some of his oratory. "The Tory pause in our forward march must be ended," said Pearson. "Confidence both at home and abroad in the future of Canada and Canada's place in the world must be restored." When it came to confidence, the voters had only recently lost confidence in the Liberal party as a place to repose it.

In the same speech Pearson also said, "I'm quite sure that I'll make some mistakes, but if I do I can promise you they will be honest mistakes for which I won't have to apologize to my conscience." He was more prophetic than he could have guessed.

One of the announcements made at the convention was that St. Laurent would yield the post of leader of the Opposition to Pearson on the following Monday. It was also made known to the press that over the weekend the new leader would consult with party executives to decide on the Liberal Party's tactical attitude toward the Diefenbaker government.

St. Laurent had followed a policy of not challenging the Tories. Stunned by the popular verdict of 1957, he stated his policy to be one of giving the new government every chance to perform its duties without opposition from the Liberals. This meant waiving the Opposition's right to offer motions of no-confidence.

No-confidence motions are more or less routine attempts by an opposition, especially at the opening of a new Parliament, to test the mettle of a government. The first duty of a party accepting the task of governing Canada is to establish that it has the confidence of the House of Commons. This may come when it wins approval of a motion endorsing the Speech from the Throne, or—as is more often the case—when it beats down an opposition amendment holding that the program outlined in the speech is inadequate or incorrect and that the government lacks the confidence of the House. Especially when a new government has taken power as a minority is it a standard gambit for the opposition to move "no confidence" in the hope of removing it immediately from office.

A change in party leadership was the logical moment for a change in Liberal tactics toward the government, if indeed the St. Laurent policy of tacit acquiescence in what Diefenbaker was doing was to be abandoned. It was a problem that concerned all the party officials regardless of who won the leadership. Some favored continuance of the laissez-faire policy, others thought the party should become more aggressive.

Pearson himself had pondered deeply on the problem. Before the convention began, consulting chiefly with his personal advisers, he had come to the provisional conclusion that it would be unwise immediately to challenge the Diefenbaker government on a confidence vote. At Pearson's request, his advisers had drafted for him an outline of a first speech in the House of Commons, if Pearson became the leader. The speech made clear that Pearson would not move no-confidence or attempt to force an election in the middle of winter, when a functioning government was needed to deal with the problem of rising unemployment; but he put the government on notice that the challenge would be made soon if it failed to tackle the issue of creating jobs.

Pearson was at work on his acceptance speech in a room in the Chateau Laurier on Thursday morning of convention week when his former cabinet colleague, J. W. Pickersgill, called on him with a new idea respecting the proper policy for the party to follow in the House.

Pickersgill was a man of waspish parliamentary skill and frequently unorthodox turns of mind. His plan called for putting the party on the offensive again but at the same time avoiding another election since the country had been through one only seven months previously. He proposed submitting a motion simply calling on the government to resign. If the motion carried, Diefenbaker and his cabinet would have to quit but the governor general could invite Pearson, as head of the second largest bloc in the House, to form a government.

Pearson was getting advice from all sides. He remarked to his next visitor, "Jack has just made an interesting suggestion. It strikes me as a bit too clever. I'll have to think about it." In any case, his acceptance speech came before that had to be decided. Some thought he should go for a motion that would force an election. Some of Pearson's personal friends were dubious about the Pickersgill plan, feeling like Pearson that it was "too clever by half," but its support by the professional politicians tended to inhibit their counsel. One close friend recalls that when he heard about the plan on that Sunday he was tempted to telephone Pearson to urge against it, but desisted under the feeling that the older politicians were the best ones to advise on a matter of political tactics.

By the time the House met at two thirty Monday afternoon, January 20, 1958, the advice of the old hands had prevailed and Pearson had his motion ready. Proceedings began with Diefenbaker paying tribute to St. Laurent on his retirement and welcoming Pearson on his assumption of the post of leader of the Opposition.

"May I say this," said Diefenbaker after reviewing Pearson's previous posts in public life. "His service has been distinguished. His opportunities for service are greatly increased as a result of the responsibility which has now come to him. Honorable members would not expect me to say more than this: that I wish him health and happiness; I wish for him the opportunity to make that contribution which he is now in a position to make in the days ahead. I congratulate him, and extend to him my best wishes in that regard."

Gracefully acknowledging the welcome, Pearson replied: "Perhaps there is no more dramatic indication of the difference between our system of free parliamentary government and that of communist totalitarian rule than the position I now hold as leader of Her Majesty's Loyal Opposition. I have, for instance, this afternoon been the recipient of the good wishes of those to whose removal from office I am dedicated. I am even now the recipient of a salary from the Crown to encourage me in that laudable and practical endeavor. If as leader of the opposition—and this is another happy contrast with communist traditions and practices—I lose my head, it will be only in a political and temperamental, not in a physical sense."

Then the House got down to its regular business, and Finance Minister Donald Fleming moved his supply motion. Pearson was on his feet at once, serving notice that the new man was going to depart from the peaceful-coexistence policy of St. Laurent.

It is customary for a leader to save his motion for introduction at the end of his speech, and Pearson devoted himself for some time to the shortcomings of the Diefenbaker government. Seven months in office, he argued, had been long enough to bring forward legislation to cure the ailing

146

economy, but the only new move it had made was in the field of trade, "and what is new there has been a sorry disappointment." Pearson claimed that trade had ceased to expand; investment was declining, tending to increase unemployment; the farmers were caught in a price squeeze; and national defense policy was "in utter confusion and contradiction."

"In view of all these things," said Pearson, "it is our view that His Excellency's advisers should, in the interest of this House of Commons, submit their resignations." But he made clear his motion was "not designed to bring on an immediate election." He was only asking the government to let him become prime minister without an election.

Across the green-carpeted aisle, John Diefenbaker listened in astonishment. Finance Minister Fleming called out: "Mike, it is sad to see you come to this." Trade and Commerce Minister George Hees flung a challenge: "We would beat the pants off you, and you know it." There was parliamentary precedent in British and Canadian history for Pearson's choice of motions, but politically it was unwise.

A few days later, Pearson confessed to a close friend he knew the instant he got to his feet that he had chosen the wrong course. And as he spoke in the House, the misgivings he had felt originally showed through his remarks. He was not, like Diefenbaker, a legal pleader, trained to ignore all facts tending to derogate from the argument he wanted to make and to concentrate only on the facts that supported it. Pearson always felt obliged to weigh the cons against the pros to achieve a judgment. He confessed candidly that there were arguments in favor of an election that appealed to him, "but I ask the honorable gentlemen opposite this: do they think that an election at this particular moment would help to solve the unemployment problem? Or would it delay for two or two and one-half months the action which is necessary and which should be taken at this time? An election at this time—and it may come, and if it comes we will be ready for it—would perhaps not help us to get back on the road of expanding trade and expanding investment; it would prolong and perhaps, during the period of an election campaign, intensify the uncertainty and the fear for the future which now exists."

No such doubts assailed John Diefenbaker about his own tactics as he cut Pearson's argument to ribbons. The first tactical objective of a new government taking power as a minority is to seek the right kind of an issue on which it can go to the people again, exploiting the psychology of its own recent success and the demoralization of the opposition under defeat, in the hope of coming out with majority status. The prime minister felt Pearson was creating just such an opportunity for him.

With all the histrionics of a practiced stump speaker and pleader at the bar, Diefenbaker lit into the Liberals for having "emerged from their recent convention full of inspiration but lacking courage."

"Now their leader moves a motion containing pusillanimous provisions and carefully designed to give the appearance that the government is afraid of a courageous stand," said Diefenbaker. "The amendment is worded as it is because my honorable friends opposite quake when they think of what will happen if an election comes." He attacked not only the strategy but the meat of Pearson's argument, producing what he described as a "hidden report" made for the St. Laurent government that warned of bad times ahead.

148

The Liberal applause for Pearson's speech had turned to heckling as Diefenbaker replied, but it began to quiet down as the Tory prime minister read excerpts citing one economic danger sign after another. The report in question was a confidential analysis of economic prospects drafted by Mitchell Sharp, then deputy minister of trade and commerce, for the government's guidance. Diefenbaker ended dramatically by tabling the document for anyone's inspection, charging that the Liberals had concealed the facts from the people.

As a maneuver designed to attract sufficient splinter-party votes to defeat the Conservatives, the Pearson motion failed. The minor-faction leaders quickly made plain they were not disposed to hand the prime ministry to Pearson on a platter.

"We could no more vote for this amendment as it stands with this proposal in it," said CCF Leader M. J. Coldwell, "than we could do anything else that appeared as unintelligent as that would be." Social Credit Leader Solon Low added: "I am not sure that he really expected us or anybody else in the opposition to take it seriously or be prepared to vote for it." Low went on to give Pearson some fatherly advice: "In the next few years you are going to hear a lot of things that will be hard to take and which you will find disconcerting. What you have to do is just sort of roll with the punches and not let it bother you too much."

The motion was voted down 150 to 95.

In the two weeks following the incident Diefenbaker surveyed public reaction and decided that the time was indeed ripe for consolidating his political position through another election. He dissolved the House and called an election for March 31. The result was a slaughter. The Liberals sank from the 105 seats they had after June 10, 1957, to 48. The

Conservatives swelled their ranks from 112 to an unprecedented majority of 208.

Even before the campaign began, Pearson remarked to a friend: "I don't know whether I'll ever be any good as leader, but one thing is sure: no leader ever made a bigger mistake at the outset of his term. It was a terrible thing." It had two bad effects immediately. It shattered party morale at a time when morale was already low, disheartening the Liberals just as they were being forced to fight a national election campaign. It made Pearson look inept and incompetent just as he took over the leadership.

It was a dreary campaign. With few people to help him, he traveled across Canada in the depth of its rigorous winter. The party organization, as it had existed while the Liberals were in office, had just about disappeared. It was typical of Pearson, however, that on the morning after his crushing defeat he wired to one of the comparatively small band who had worked most devotedly for him: "I am just as grateful as I would have been if the result had been reversed."

But in national politics, as in international affairs, the changes produced by dramatic events such as this often carry the seeds of longer-range developments that are not apparent in the immediate assessment of what has happened. From this standpoint the ordeal had two beneficial results for Mike Pearson. It taught him at the very beginning that he could not do worse as leader by following his own instincts than by listening to the advice of the "professional" politicians. And in a "silver lining" sense, defeat at the nadir of party fortunes eliminated the old guard and left him free to recruit new blood in his effort to rebuild an effective new Liberal opposition.

11

Calling All Eggheads

HOW DOES one go about rebuilding a national political party that has been crushed at the polls, especially one so thoroughly crushed as were the Liberals in 1958?

The normal reaction of the politician who has any heart left in him is to think in terms of organization, rebuilding from the grass roots. He looks for a Jim Farley or Leonard Hall—or, in Canada, a man like Diefenbaker's Allister Grosart—whose consuming interest is organizational politics and for whom the contest for votes is the most absorbing of occupations; who travels the country exhorting the faithful, promoting improvement of constituency units and compiling information on issues that might attract voters next time; a man who, when at headquarters, spends what seems like twenty-four hours a day on the long-distance telephone getting regional opinion, patching up organizational problems, and soothing ruffled feelings. Successful political campaigns always seem to turn up one politician's politician, a man seemingly incapable of any personal political ideology yet at the same time supremely convinced that only his own party can save the country from ruin, and capable for all his partisanship of coldly objective analytical calculation of the voters' whims.

Such personalities are generally looked down on by the average intellectual or semi-intellectual as belonging to a caste rather low on the social scale. The man or woman entering politics with some feeling of idealism regards the politician as conniving and unreliable. It usually comes as a surprise to him to learn that a man with this type of organizational genius often turns out, on closer acquaintance, to have more to his character than one would suspect; that he is a man of his word, and that within the code of politics his rating for integrity is high. The idealist, tending to expect the worst of a politician and suspicious of being double-crossed at any moment, forgets that a politician's good faith is his only real stock in trade.

Grosart, a successful Toronto advertising man who masterminded strategy and organization for Diefenbaker's first two campaigns, was a cultured man with an appreciation of Chinese and Canadian art, and an enthusiastic amateur gardener. He possessed a penetrating insight into the essentials of the task he had taken on. The product he wanted to sell the Canadian people was John Diefenbaker, and all considerations of his political activity were examined in the light of that primary objective. He knew Diefenbaker's mind better than anyone else. He knew that newspapermen are, in the main, small "l" liberals, being usually younger than most of the political figures with whom they deal, tending to be intellectuals, and lacking the span of experience which invariably injects some measure of small "c" conservatism into individuals of whatever political label. He knew the value of honest talk with newsmen, regardless of their personal predictions or the political outlook of their papers. Canadian politics being the relatively informal process it is, compared to the machine-ridden U.S., it wasn't till Grosart appeared on the scene that the party organizer became a figure of substance in Canada. Until Grosart was given appointment to the Senate in 1962, the appointment of a national organizer was good for no more than a routine paragraph on an inside page of most newspapers, but when his promotion created a vacancy at Progressive-Conservative headquarters in Ottawa it was a subject of major speculation who might replace him.

Pearson was not a normal politician, and in any case there was no Liberal Grosart immediately in sight. Pearson's course was to take counsel of his closest friends. Among them were Walter Gordon, his old associate of Royal Commission days, now a partner in the Toronto firm of Clarkson, Gordon & Co., chartered accountants, and in Woods, Gordon & Co., management consultants; Maurice LaMontagne, economist and professor; Robert Fowler, president of the Canadian Pulp and Paper Association in Montreal; and Tom Kent; none of these was a "politician."

As he talked to these and other friends a typically Pearsonian idea began to form in his mind: what was needed was a re-examination of the philosophical basis of the Liberal Party. It had got away from Liberal principles in its long years in power, and was thinking on the lower level of political expediency.

One day in the spring of 1960 Pearson telephoned his friend

Mitchell Sharp in Toronto. Sharp, after the 1958 election, had resigned his top civil service post at the Department of Trade and Commerce and was a vice-president of Brazilian Traction. Pearson told him he wanted him to do a job and would talk to him about it next time he was in Toronto.

Shortly afterward they met at Toronto's Park Plaza Hotel and Pearson detailed what he had in mind. He wanted Sharp to organize a conference of liberal-minded Canadians—not Liberals—who would discuss what the policies of a liberal Canadian political party should be. Those were the only instructions; would Sharp undertake to select such a group?

Sharp did. First he organized a sponsoring committee, comprising leading liberals not prominent as party figures. They included such people as Walter Gordon, Robert Fowler, newspaper publisher Victor Sifton, Carleton University President A. Davidson Dunton. Then with the help of Michael Mackenzie, a young associate of Gordon's, Sharp brought together a small group of young men and women who compiled a list of topics that might be discussed and prepared a program. The plan was to have a series of speakers, specialists in their fields, read papers on the selected topics and then open them to discussion. Not one politician was among the speakers; nor was the conference to be limited to people who voted Liberal. One of the participants was historian Frank Underhill, who had been a member of the Commonwealth Co-operative Federation, which later joined with organized labor to become the New Democratic Party. Some Liberal politicians attended, including several former ministers of the Crown, defeated and undefeated, but their role was to sit and listen. None was on the program, except J. W. Pickersgill, who was assigned to do a summing up at the close as one of three who

154

would pull together the thoughts advanced during the discussions. It was to be an invitation conference, not a free-for-all meeting. Those invited paid twenty-five dollars for the privilege and took care of their own expenses. Also, the original intention was that it would be private, so that participants could kick ideas around with a frankness not possible in the presence of the press. Some of the conference papers were prepared on that understanding: they aimed to be provocative and to generate discussion, not necessarily to suggest policy lines for the party.

There was, however, great pressure from the press to be permitted coverage. Sharp and the other sponsors eventually decided—almost on the eve of the meeting—that unless news-media representatives were admitted, garbled versions of what went on would get out. As a result the rules were changed to permit full press coverage of the opening speeches and to let the newsmen sit in and report the tenor of the discussions on condition that they not quote directly from, or identify, the speakers who took part in the extemporaneous comment on the papers.

Another change that had an effect on the character of the meeting as originally planned was expansion of the invitation list by about double. In all some two hundred attended, and even at that, an equal number who wanted to go could not be accommodated.

The shifting of ground rules on the matter of publicity abashed some of the men who had prepared papers. Tom Kent, for one, was so appalled that he was on the verge of stalking out when, on arrival, he discovered the change. He felt that his paper, "Toward a Philosophy of Social Security," was not the kind of thing to be unveiled in a political context where it would inevitably be interpreted in terms of current party policy.

The conference convened at Queen's University in Kingston, Ontario, on September 6, 1960, and lasted the rest of the week—five strenuous days of intense discussion. "The meetings never ended," Sharp said later. "Talk went on all the time, wherever we met, and I didn't get to bed before 2 A.M. any night."

In his introductory remarks Sharp explained the purpose: "This conference has been organized primarily to give the politicians an opportunity of listening to what the non-politicians have to say about certain major national problems. Put less politely, your brains are to be picked." He said that from reading the manuscripts submitted in advance, the meeting obviously was not going to be a mutual-admiration society. "I'm tempted to say that any semblance between the views of the speakers and the views of Liberal spokesmen is purely coincidental."

The object, he went on, was not to criticize the Diefenbaker administration, nor to write a platform for the Liberal party—the conferees would not be asked to reach conclusions or subscribe to resolutions. "Nevertheless, this conference has a definite and a serious purpose, which I have no hesitation whatever in stating. It is to discover what a group of intelligent, well-informed, liberally minded Canadians from all walks of life and all parts of the country think ought to be done about some of the more serious national problems."

Pearson, who gave the opening address, put it much the same: "We are here to study national problems in their political context; to see what we can do about them through political action based on sound political thought." At the outset, however, he had some remarks about politics, wonderfully revealing of his attitude toward the profession into which, with some reluctance, he had been drawn:

"Politics, of course, has become, if not a bad word, at least one which does not at once conjure up a vision of devoted, unselfish service to one's fellow man.

"It is the most important of all secular callings; yet it is one in which many men and women of integrity and ability scorn to participate actively. It is considered as a rather unworthy pursuit; like running a confidence game or managing a prize fighter in New York.

"In a Gallup Poll several years ago in the United States, a result was obtained which showed that all mothers wanted their sons to grow up to be President, but 73 per cent didn't want them to become politicians in the process.

"They apparently expected—or at least hoped—that their presidential sons would spring, like Athena, fully equipped from the brain of Jove . . .

"Politics is not magic, black or otherwise. It is certainly not an exact science, and the material with which it operates, human nature, precludes it from ever becoming one. There is no way by which, in politics, a calculation can be made in such a precise form as to ensure a predicted result; even in voting.

"Politics is an art. I have heard it called the adaptation and administration of the unintended. Sometimes it is the art of adjusting to the inevitable with the minimum of disturbance—economic, social, or electoral. Nearly always it is the art of using effectively and skillfully, blunt instruments, including, especially, public opinion. It is, above all, the search for compromise without betrayal; which involves

157

the recurring risk of inconsistency and requires, as Sir Winston Churchill put it so appealingly, ensuring that one's 'views are a harmonious process which keeps them in tune with the current of events.'

"Good politics is, above all, service—and not to self. If it becomes self-service, it is degrading, and the practitioner's immediate success—for this kind of politics can have temporary success—will not for long prevent or conceal ultimate and lasting failure ...

"As we enter a new decade, the decade of outer space, the decade of the dispossessed, the decade of choice between peaceful progress or total destruction, the problems we face both nationally and internationally (they can no longer be neatly separated) are quite unprecedented.

"I suppose men have been saying this about every new decade since the birth of political society; that its problems were unprecedented. But we can certainly say it now with complete, if discouraging, assurance; for our problems have indeed reached new dimensions. We are in outer space and in inner turmoil; we have both cobalt bombs and hydrogen bombs. We can communicate with a satellite 25 million miles away, but not with a human across a curtain. We can spread political power throughout the nation, but we cannot be sure of its responsible exercise.

"These new developments of revolutionary importance which have taken place have a meaning for politics in a democratic society, a meaning which is often obscured by our obsession with old ideas and practices and prejudices; and with shibboleths that have lost their meaning ... In this new decade, political liberalism will be meaningless and irrelevant unless it produces policies and solutions that make sense in terms of today's problems and today's opportunities."

He then listed some of the problems on which he sought answers:

The "problem of work"—"Unemployment is our major cause for domestic concern."

National development—"The vision of arctic development [which had been a subject of Diefenbaker spellbinding] is a stimulating and exciting one to every Canadian. But is it to be given a priority even higher than the redevelopment of the Atlantic provinces [chronically depressed in comparison with other sections of the country] which have for so long made such a magnificent contribution to the development of other parts of Canada?"

International trade—"Recent European developments have a major significance for us of which we don't seem to be sufficiently aware. Why aren't we trying harder to convert a European free-trade area into an Atlantic free-trade area? Why did we spurn—as unworthy of a second glance—the offer of freer trade made by the United Kingdom?" He was alluding to Diefenbaker's announced intention to divert 15 per cent of Canada's U.S. trade to the U.K., countered by Britain's offer to consider a free-trade agreement with her former dominion, an offer which Canada rejected.

Trade with the U.S.—"The dependence of Canada on the United States market for trade and on United States capital for development is an increasing threat to our independence ... But, if we lose our national purpose and identity, it will be by our own default, not by the design of anybody else."

National defense—"With the advent of intercontinental nuclear missiles and with our entry into outer space, everything changed, especially for smaller powers. Canadian policy has not changed with it . . . Canada gets no defense, in the literal territorial sense, from what we are now doing. Our only defense is peace. But we are not—as a middle power—making the kind of contribution we should or could be making, through our defense or foreign policies, to the peace."

Agriculture—"The cost-price squeeze is the label put on the complex set of forces influencing the standard of prosperity in agriculture. This label itself does not explain, or even indicate, that there is a revolution going on in agriculture—in Canada and the world; that it is one as far-reaching in its significance as the industrial revolution of the eighteenth century . . . New ways must be found of dealing with this particular phase of the agricultural problems which would apply with equal force to subsistence occupations in the fisheries and forestry."

Social security—"The real issue is how to carry forward the further improvements in our present system which are required without undermining the freedom and initiative of the individual and the capacity of our resources to sustain such improvements."

Labor—"There is no point in viewing Labor today in the context of the struggles for the recognition of trade unionism itself. The sensible approach is to view modern unionism as a new power in the social structure with an established place in our economic life. With that view firmly in mind, it should then be possible to discuss how the economic and social goals of unionism can best be harmonized with the public interest."

He concluded that for the future, applying his personal creed to the party, liberalism in Canada "should expect only one thing: an opportunity to serve our country once again in the responsibility of office; an opportunity which, by its policies and its performance, it must earn, for this is the only way by which power deserves to be gained or retained."

With these propositions for a start, the intellectuals assembled at Kingston churned up the yeastiest brew of political opinions Canada had experienced for many a year. Many principal speakers expressed views diametrically at variance with each other.

James Eayrs, a young, tough-minded professor from the University of Toronto, read a paper outlining a proposed defense policy for Canada. Picturing Canada as the only country it would be impossible for Russia to attack without provoking massive retaliation by the United States, and also the only country incapable of contracting out of a major nuclear war if one occurred, he judged there was no strategic justification for Canada attempting to acquire her own nuclear deterrent. Hence, he reasoned, it was to Canada's own direct interest to increase the effectiveness of the great deterrent under U.S. control—the nuclear weapons capable of delivery by the Strategic Air Command in retaliation for attack.

He saw four ways in which this could be done: 1) by opening Canadian territory to bases for U.S. retaliatory missiles; 2) by permitting the U.S. to set up antimissile and antiaircraft defenses in Canada; 3) by improving civil defense and treating it as a major component of national security policy; and 4) by improving political communication between the communist world and ours, "with the object of removing its fear of surprise attack as an inducement to pre-emptive strategy."

Toward the last objective he conceded that Canada's scope of action was more limited than that of the United States, but he suggested that Ottawa could invite Communist China to open a diplomatic mission in the hope it would "afford the communist world better insight into ours and logically lessen tension between the two." If Canada permitted establishment of U.S. bases, she should "insist" on her intention to permit Soviet observers to inspect them, and not only the U.S. bases but Canadian bases, Bomarc sites, and radar warning lines. "The risks of sabotage must be acknowledged and reckoned with," he said, "but it should be possible to devise procedures by which these may be made inconsequential."

Eayrs introduced some ivory-tower thinking that was characteristic of some of the conference as he went on to make some wildly impractical suggestions designed to cure the Russians of fear that the West wanted to make war on them:

"If inspecting weapons systems offers no assurance to the Russians that we are not planning to use them offensively against them, it may be to our advantage to let them scrutinize our operational orders. This might mean—to take an extreme example—admitting Marshal Malinovsky to meetings of our cabinet defense committee. Still more effective—and more extreme—would be to turn over to the Soviet Union an equal number of the kind of weapons whose offensive capabilities they most greatly feared, providing us with the assurance of their assurance that a Western pre-emptive strike would be deterred by knowledge of the certainty of Soviet retaliation." Only by actions as heroic as these, Eayrs argued, could Canada "live as safely as possible with our atomically armed duelist across the North Pole."

Much more down to earth was the paper of Michael Barkway, then Ottawa correspondent for the *Toronto Star* and now publisher of the *Financial Times of Canada*. It also was the most devastating critique on past Liberal policy read at the conference. Under the title "How Independent Can We Be?" Barkway discussed mostly Canada's need to preserve a separate economic identity from the U.S., but he covered defense questions in passing and differed radically with Eayrs.

"We are now very near the end of the period when it could be said that the defense of Canada and the United States was inseparable," said Barkway. "It was never more than a partial truth. Present NORAD plans have never been designed for the defense of Canada, which is impossible and also unnecessary—except insofar as bombers failing to reach their targets in the U.S. might unload over Canada either by mistake or as providing better-than-nothing secondary targets."

Barkway held that as soon as the ICBM definitely replaced the manned bomber, "Canada is off the hook." At that point, he argued, "we shall be, for practical purposes, the most detached instead of the most involved of the NATO allies. Strategically, apart from our obligations to NATO, we shall be in the same position as one of the Latin American republics."

Barkway's main theme, however, was that Canadians had only themselves to blame if they permitted the U.S. to absorb them economically. The great aberration of the 1950s—when Liberal governments were in office and C. D. Howe the power behind them—was, he said, "cringing passivity" in the face of an overwhelming flood of American investment.

"I am, I think, among the least anti-American people I know," said Barkway. "I have never blamed the American government, nor American business, nor American society for the fact that American influence and American economic control are, as I believe, too predominant in Canada. There is no possible excuse for blaming them. American business is doing what comes naturally. If we leave a vacuum waiting for them to fill, they have every right not only to exploit the opportunity but even to assume that we want them to exploit it. [American] patience often amazes me. Nothing could be more unfair than the demands of those who make a fetish of not being anti-American. What they say is: 'We won't stand up for ourselves, but we expect you to take great care not to offend our susceptibilities. And please remember that our susceptibilities are very tender.' " Barkway said he "loathed this trick" of passing the buck to Americans; that "from the history of the 1950's, we can only conclude that Canada puts its independence several places down on its list of values." Canada has survived "only by matching the power of the state against the power of foreign capital," and "whenever the Canadian government ceases to assert itself resolutely and purposefully against the big millions, Canada's national survival is in jeopardy."

Barkway conceded that abrupt termination of all foreign investment "would be like depriving a drug addict of his heroin." He thought the problem had to be handled gently and gradually, by first making changes in tax policy, such as changing depreciation and depletion allowances to favor Canadian enterprises against American and forcing publication of the accounts of foreign-owned subsidiaries and branch plants. Beyond that he proposed revision of the U.S.-Canadian tax treaty and its abrogation if satisfactory changes could not be negotiated.

But just as Barkway had differed with Eayrs on defense, Harry G. Johnson, one of the best-known Canadian economists, whose reputation was built first in England and then at the University of Chicago, differed with Barkway on economics. Johnson spoke on the implications for Canada of the European Common Market. Said Johnson:

"In concrete terms, the choice is between resisting the trend toward closer integration with the U.S. and making a definite move to confirm and accelerate it. Economically, it seems to me, the arguments for integration with the United States are overwhelming; and for reasons that I have already touched on, I do not believe that integration with the American economy would constitute any threat to Canadian independence.

"Specifically, I propose that Canada should seek to negotiate reciprocal free trade with the United States. I suggest a free trade area rather than a customs union or more comprehensive economic union embracing coordination of economic policies and planning because, while a free trade area requires a customs check on the origin of goods crossing the frontier and a set of rules defining the origin of goods made with imported components, whereas a customs or wider union raises no such administrative problems, it leaves much more latitude to members in their dealings with other countries—a freedom which does seem to me an essential of Canadian independence." He conceded that replacement of protection by free trade would lead to some "radical changes in the structure of Canadian industry," but had various reasons for contending it would "not drastically alter the balance of the Canadian economy as between manufacturing and other activities, or even the relative importance of various industries."

With such vigorously dissenting opinions on how to better Canada's lot, and no attempt at consensus, it is no wonder that Diefenbaker and the Conservative strategists were completely baffled by the eggheads at Kingston. Inclined to believe that the Liberals had committed a serious error by exposing themselves to such criticism, the Tories combed through the speeches looking for political footholds. Among the few Diefenbaker was able to find was a proposal by Tom Kent that advertising be taxed, "like liquor or gasoline or thousands of other more useful things." Diefenbaker cited this item out of Kent's paper, together with an endorsement of the idea in a paper on "Growth, Price Stability, and the Problem of Unemployment" by Maurice LaMontagne, as evidence of socialistic tendencies in the Liberal ranks. In a speech in the House of Commons he also coupled their names with that of Sharp to charge that the party was run by "bureaucrats" who wanted to run the country. It was a charge he repeated in subsequent campaigns, but the fact was that only Sharp, as a former deputy minister, could be accurately described as a "bureaucrat."

Perhaps the only effect of the conference on the Canadian political scene was to spread the idea that intellectuals were behind the Liberal party. Harold Greer, of the *Toronto Globe & Mail,* one of those who covered the event, wrote in his paper:

"Kingston was an egghead conference, and Mr. Pearson— a one time professor and long-time diplomat—is something of an egghead himself. The intellectual is by definition engrossed in ideas, and the great trouble with him is that he tends to pursue an idea not to a decision but to another idea, and so on ad infinitum.

"The politician, however, must think with his liver . . . Between the intellectual and the politician there is a constant quarrel because the intellectual begins by saying he doesn't know, an admission which is fatal for the politician."

12

The Offensive Begins

EVEN THOUGH the Kingston conference itself failed to produce any sharp crystallization of Liberal thinking, new ideas did begin to filter into the Liberal platform. They took shape at a party rally held in Ottawa in January, 1961.

To anyone accustomed to the cynical professionalism of the U.S. political convention, the Canadian political rally is a charmingly ingenuous institution. The look of Canadian politics is, on the surface, very much like the look of American politics. The nomenclature is, of course, different. In the U.S. a candidate might run for the House of Representatives from the fourth district of Ohio, and while the Constitution does not require that he live within its boundaries, rare indeed is the politician who can win election without at least some claim to local residence. In Canada the constituency units, usually called *ridings,* bear individual names; the member elected to Parliament will be recognized to speak as "the honorable member from St. Jean-Iberville-Napierville," not as "the gentleman from Quebec." And though the majority of members do live in their own ridings, it is by no means insisted on. In 1962 the New Democratic Party leader, T. C. Douglas, re-entering federal politics after seventeen years as premier of Saskatchewan, lost his bid for the House of Commons in his home riding of Weyburn but was provided with a seat by the resignation of a loyal NDP member in Burnaby-Coquitlam, a "safe" NDP constituency halfway across the continent in British Columbia. Douglas ran for this seat, and he won in a by-election. But Canadian electioneering is rather similar to that which takes place south of the border. The House of Commons in session looks and acts remarkably like the House of Representatives, with a bit of the U.S. Senate's atmosphere added. Commons is the more important of the two chambers that make up the Canadian Parliament; the Senate is an appointive body like the British House of Lords, treated with great respect but relatively impotent.

On the surface a national political rally bears something of the look of a U.S. political convention, with delegates, banners, placards, resolutions committees, speeches, motions from the floor, shouting, noise, and general disordered zeal. A Canadian "nominating convention" differs from a "rally," since in addition to passing resolutions the party picks a "leader." If the party wins most seats in the next federal election, the leader gets to be prime minister, provided he wins his own constituency; yet it is not the same thing as nominating an individual for prime minister. He is not voted on for the job by the people of Canada as a whole, only by the electors in his own riding. Electors in other ridings can express their support of him only indirectly, by voting for the local candidate belonging to the same party.

National nominating conventions, however, are held only when the leadership post becomes vacant for one reason or another, and when a leader like Mackenzie King holds sway for twenty-five years, they are few and far between. Nor are they preludes to an election. Consequently some instrument is needed to generate party enthusiasm on a regular basis, and the "rally," by one name or another, held annually or biennially is the answer.

The Liberals' 1961 rally was not, therefore, a meeting Pearson needed for re-election as leader, but solely a gathering called to re-examine party policy by passing resolutions. Its proceedings were all held in the open and its discussions were all about policy, so that it had a good deal of the democratic character of a town meeting. It was not so totally amateur, however, that there was no back-of-the-scenes influence. Pearson turned the job of policy guidance over to his good friend Walter Gordon, who with Tom Kent's aid provided firm guidance for the shaping of the resolutions.

"People got down to fairly strenuous arguments about the policy issues that were of main interest to them as individuals," Gordon recalls. "This made it clear to the leaders of the Liberal party what their more articulate followers felt and wanted. There was a lull after the rally for a few months, mainly because everybody had worked up to a pitch, but it became quite clear what the younger element, the more progressive element, thought Liberal Party should stand for. This was very useful to Mr. Pearson and everybody else. I think it probably confirmed his own views.

"People came to crab and complain and they went away thoroughly enthusiastic and dedicated. The fact that it was such a tremendous rally gave Mr. Pearson and his group in the House of Commons a great lift, a feeling that they did have a pretty interesting and pretty able lot of people behind them in the country. I think it had a lot to do with their improved spirit in the months that followed."

Political resolutions are invariably full of platitudes and are tediously repetitious from year to year. The 1961 Liberal resolutions were no exception to this rule, repeating most of the concepts on which the party had run and lost in 1958; but a few new planks were added to the platform. The new ideas that made their appearance then look more significant now, after the Pearson government put some of them into action when it assumed power.

In connection with their old emphasis on the need for getting the burden of unemployment off the back of the Canadian economy, the Liberals argued that there was no one cure for it. A comprehensive program was needed, they stated, including special recognition of the needs of depressed areas, where established industries had declined in the face of changing manufacturing patterns and new ones had not come forward to take their place. The Liberals proposed special tax incentives to attract new businesses, promised to make more credit available, and offered to finance power and transport developments. After taking power, the Pearson government attempted to carry out this policy in a number of ways. Finance Minister Walter Gordon's budget offered three-year tax holidays for new industries started in economically stagnating areas, and a special fund of $100,000,000 was voted to foster development in the four Atlantic provinces, which for years had lagged behind the rest of the country.

In 1961 the party reflected Canadian concern about the increasing control by foreigners over Canadian industry. It proposed encouraging Canadian ownership by tax incentives; by revision of regulations governing the investment of pension, trust, insurance and other institutional funds; and by a national propaganda program to "reshape the attitude of Canadians to investment of savings." After assuming power, the Liberals took action in this area, too. Most spectacular, and most disastrous, was Gordon's inclusion in the 1963-64 budget of a 30 per cent tax on sales of Canadian securities to foreigners. It had such an immediate and unsettling effect on the securities market that within a week Gordon had to withdraw it, with enormous political loss of face. In another move toward economic repatriation, the government introduced legislation to set up a Canada Development Corporation, seeking to give individual citizens and institutional investors a chance to buy shares in a company that would pool their money for use in financing Canadian development enterprises and in buying Canadian firms that might otherwise sell out to foreigners.

Perhaps the most significant innovation of 1961, however, was a Liberal resolution to let provinces "contract out" of federal-provincial programs. The significance of this requires a bit of elaboration.

As brought into being in 1867, the Canadian Confederation envisioned a strong central government. The framers of confederation had the United States Civil War fresh in their minds as an example of the defects of a "states' rights" system with checks and balances; in the British North America Act the powers not granted to the provinces were reserved for the central government, which also had its enumerated powers. This was the precise reverse of the American Constitution. However, a series of judicial decisions by the Imperial Privy Council in London from 1896 onward had the effect of nullifying the federal government's reserve power except in case of great emergency, such as war. The provinces became, in some ways, the equals of the central government. But most of the taxing power had been vested with the Dominion. Thus as the twentieth century brought a trend toward social legislation, much of which required national application to be truly effective, the provinces found themselves with the authority but not the money, and the Dominion with the means but not the power. While this system enabled the central government to meet the demands of two world wars, under the decision of the empire's highest court * even the economic emergency of the depression of the 1930's was not great enough to invoke the Dominion's overriding powers. Power flowed to the central government in war, and ebbed to the provinces in peace. Ever since 1946, when tax agreements made with the provinces for the purpose of waging war came to an end, there has been dispute between Ottawa and the provinces over the proper way to implement and pay

* In its glacially slow evolution of independence from Great Britain, Canada did not abolish appeals to the Privy Council in London until 1949. Only two years previously, in 1947, did it establish Canadian citizenship as something apart from the status of British subject. There is one remaining vestige of British control: Canada cannot even now amend its own constitution, but must request the British Parliament to change it. By custom this is always done at Canada's request, but "repatriating the constitution" remains a political objective, requiring the consent of the provinces to accomplish, and resisted so far by Quebec, which fears giving the English provinces authority over the amending process.

for social programs such as pensions and unemployment insurance.

The 1961 Liberal resolution favored regular consultation with the provinces "to ensure that priorities in the use of taxes are kept constantly in line with changing conditions and in order to ensure that the provincial governments have adequate revenues to provide their citizens an adequate standard of services and to perform their constitutional obligations." It noted that several programs, including disability pensions, which had been started on a basis of sharing the costs between the federal and provincial governments, had been established throughout Canada. "In these cases," said the resolution, "a new Liberal government will be happy to leave the field entirely to the provinces, and to evolve appropriate readjustments in its taxes, so as to provide for full provincial financing."

The policy thus enunciated had its test after the Pearson government took office. Quebec and Ontario objected to Ottawa's $400,000,000 municipal-loan fund, designed to stimulate public works and provide employment, on the ground that municipalities were the exclusive creatures of the provinces and Ottawa was interfering in provincial affairs by dealing with them. Pearson avoided prolonged conflict over the issue by announcing at a conference with the premiers that he was willing to divide the fund in proportion to population, and agreeing that each province could contract with the federal administering board to take over administration within the province. This "contracting out" arrangement did not touch the question of readjusting the division of taxes; nor did the formula prove immediately adaptable to the much knottier problem of agreement on a Pearson government plan

173

to introduce a national system of contributory portable pensions. The pension program was an attempt to introduce in Canada a plan somewhat similar to the United States Social Security system permitting Canadians to move from a job in one province to a job in another and carry with them the equity they had built up in a fund to provide for their retirement. Quebec "contracted out" of the pension plan but put no obstacle in the path of co-operation by the other provinces.

It would seem that when Pearson got Canadians to rethink what the philosophy of a liberal party should be, inevitably the thinking was in terms of Canada as a whole rather than in terms of regional interest. And all-Canada thinking inevitably meant an attack on entrenched regional outlook.

"In some important respects, the partnership of federal and provincial governments in our confederation has to be reshaped," Pearson told the premiers at the conference on municipal loans and pensions. "What we see, looking at the situation of confederation from the point of view of Canada as a whole, is in no fundamental conflict with what you see, as you discharge your responsibilities to your respective provinces. It would be tragic if there were such a conflict. I do not believe that there is. There must not be, for if there were, Canada could disappear."

Equally, all-Canada thinking required an attempt at finding new compromises to promote provincial acceptance of the kind of authority a federal government must have in the modern world if it is to administer a country that considers itself a nation. "The responsibility we share," said Pearson to the premiers, "is responsibility for the good government of the whole of Canada. We want to work together for the preservation, progress and improvement of our Canadian con-

174

federation. That confederation is very special in the extent to which it is built on unity without uniformity. It is near to being unique in the extent to which it has been built despite great obstacles, despite pervasive and powerful pressures which would submerge our Canadian identity. The task on which we are working together is not easy. I believe we can show that it is not beyond our resources of will and understanding."

In effect it took two years of what Walter Gordon describes as "a lot of preliminary talk and threshing out of ideas" for Pearson to achieve a feeling that he and the Liberal party knew where they were going. The next step was practical reorganization. The party machinery had literally fallen to pieces after 1958. As the first step in organizing for the campaign that could come any time within the next two years, Pearson appointed two campaign managers, one a seasoned French Canadian politician, Lionel Chevrier, who had been his colleague in previous Liberal cabinets; and an amateur, Walter Gordon.

Although he had not held political office, Gordon was a wealthy management consultant with a good sense of what it took to create an organization. He began assembling a staff of a few key people to help the leader of the Opposition. Richard O'Hagan, a former newspaperman, was recruited from a Toronto advertising agency to serve as Pearson's press adviser. A new national organizer for the party was found in the person of thirty-five-year-old Keith Davey, who was now on the business staff of one of the Toronto radio stations. Davey, an immensely energetic salesman who lived and breathed politics, was chairman of the Liberal party associations for the Greater Toronto area. Tom Kent, who had left his Winnipeg paper to become a vice-president of Chemcell Limited, was hired to help write speeches and provide general braintrusting. Maurice LaMontagne, a University of Ottawa economist, was made Pearson's economic consultant. Research people were put to work for the party and the opposition leader's office. Pearson himself picked Senator John J. Connolly, an Ottawa lawyer, as president of the National Liberal Federation; among a group of team members characterized by different types of aggressiveness he supplied an Irish political charm and finesse that were an asset to the group. Allan J. MacEachen, a young man who had served in parliament from Inverness, N. S., but who had been defeated in 1958, joined the opposition staff; and Mary Macdonald, who had been Mr. Pearson's secretary for some years when he was in the Department of External Affairs, continued to play an important part as adviser on constituency affairs.

Gordon says the first thing he did, apart from finding the team of helpers for Pearson, was to make up his mind how soon the party could be ready for an election. He judged it needed a full year to get organized well enough to challenge the ruling Tories, and set his sights on getting the machine perfected for an election in June, 1962. Oddly enough—certainly not because of Gordon's planning, since naming the date was solely Prime Minister Diefenbaker's prerogative—June 18 turned out to be the date of the balloting.

"I decided," said Gordon, "that if we had to, we might be able to get ready a month or so sooner, but we had better have all our planning done by June. Afterward everybody and his brother used to come to me and say, 'you've got to be ready for September,' or October, or some other month. I just went ahead and let them talk and never changed any-

176

thing. I knew that if the election came in September, 1961, we would be badly beaten; we couldn't get ready for it in time and so there was no use chopping and changing. We just went straight ahead as if it was going to be in June, 1962. There was a scare first that it would be in the fall, and a real scare that it was going to be in March. A March election would have caught us badly. But we didn't change course, so we were essentially ready for June."

Just as the Liberals began to feel the tonic effects of rejuvenation in the summer of 1961, the Diefenbaker government made two egregious political blunders.

The first involved an attempt to oust the governor of the Bank of Canada, James E. Coyne, seven months before the expiration of his ten-year term. Central-government bankers are usually an aloof and silent lot, and therefore men who carry about them an aura of power and mystery. They operate deep down behind the scenes. Like the oracle of Delphi they sometimes speak; and when they do the markets tremble even though their speech is usually incomprehensible to the lay public.

Coyne had lately departed from this role. In a series of speeches around the country he told Canadians they were living beyond their means and were headed for disaster unless they changed their ways. He advocated a number of steps designed to reverse the trend, some of them protectionist in character. While maintaining the pretense of aloofness by refusing to be drawn into debate over his proposals, Coyne did in fact become a politically controversial figure. A group of twenty-nine university economists petitioned the government to fire him. In the House, Liberal front-benchers demanded that the government say whether it supported or repudiated Coyne's ideas, since under a system of responsible government the statements of top officials can be assumed to represent government policy unless repudiated by the prime minister.

Diefenbaker's finance minister, Donald M. Fleming, ducked the issue. He neither supported nor repudiated Coyne's line on economic policy. He contended that Coyne and the Bank of Canada were responsible to Parliament, not to the government, which may have been correct in a legal sense but was begging the question in the political sense, since the Tories controlled the House so completely.

But the day arrived when Coyne suddenly announced, after a meeting of the bank's directors in Quebec City, that the government had asked for his resignation. Coyne refused to be ousted, blowing open the biggest brawl in Canadian politics since 1956, when the Liberals under St. Laurent and C. D. Howe got caught in what became known as "the pipeline debate." Fleming's first explanation was that the government was outraged by Coyne's action in approving an increase in his own pension rights that would entitle him to $25,000 a year, instead of $12,000, on retirement. Later on, when he brought in his 1962 budget, Fleming implied that the real motive behind the government's action was a desire on the government's part to be "expansionist" in economic terms and that Coyne wanted to be "restrictionist." In view of the government's ultimate authority over the bank, and the fact that Coyne would have been out of office at the end of the year anyway, Fleming's explanation was not convincing. Walter Gordon's belief was that the Tories realized they had been making fundamental economic mistakes and wanted a scapegoat to explain a shift in policy.

Coyne not only refused to resign but claimed, successfully, that the board lacked authority to dismiss him. With characteristic arrogance he had refused, under the economists' attack, to dignify their criticism by reply; to newsmen who had managed to negotiate an appointment with him through channels he had curtly refused to answer the points of criticism or to permit quotation or attribution of what he did say. Now he became as accessible as a public telephone booth: callers who rang up the bank's number and asked for Mr. Coyne were put through to him directly, even without having to identify themselves. In his eagerness to tell his side of the story, he ground out statements on the bank's duplicating machines and made public memoranda he had submitted to Fleming. Where once he had responded to requests for news pictures by sending an official portrait complete with instructions how it should be cropped for reproduction, he now submitted on request to being photographed informally with his wife and children. He demanded a public hearing before the House banking and commerce committee.

In a country unaccustomed to such departures from public decorum, this was an incredibly sensational performance. The government made the politically fatal mistake of refusing to permit his appearance before the banking committee, which it controlled, and was left with no choice but to introduce legislation declaring his post vacant.

The situation was one which Pearson exploited adroitly. At the time his strategy seemed too subtle to be politically effective, for Pearson refused to associate himself with Coyne's economic views. His one point of attack on the government was that Coyne was entitled to the democratic right of having a hearing before he was judged. He made a slogan of the phrase that Coyne was entitled to "his day in court." Despite its subtlety, this argument carried force. Pearson was able to make it work because the Senate, still top-heavy with Liberal appointees from the long years of Mackenzie King and St. Laurent, rallied its Liberal majority to provide Coyne with the forum he was seeking. After some days of jam-packed hearings in which he got ample scope to detail his complaints of mistreatment by the government, Coyne resigned, claiming he had won vindication before the public, and retreated immediately into his former cold aloofness. The net effect of the unseemly performance was to give the Diefenbaker government an appearance of bungled administration.

While this dramatic personality row was going on, the Liberals locked horns with the government on a less spectacular but more fundamental issue. It involved a bill amending the customs act to authorize the minister of national revenue to increase import duties anywhere from 7½ to 22½ per cent, without further parliamentary authority, on goods of a "class or kind" made in Canada. As a measure designed to protect Canadian manufacturers against foreign competition at a time when unemployment was severe, it represented the restrictive legislation to which Liberals objected. In fighting the government on the issue, Pearson again operated through the upper chamber, consulting daily with the Liberal Senate leader, Ross MacDonald.

The Canadian Senate, like the British House of Lords, is expected to be gentlemanly about accepting what bills the House sends it for approval. The system indulges an occasional inoffensive Senate amendment to preserve the fiction that it is an independent body, but any serious interference with government programs brings threats of retaliation.

"Reform of the Senate" has been a frequent political threat although it is seldom defined; interpretation of its meaning has ranged from abolition of the upper chamber to forced retirement of members from their life jobs at seventy-five.

In this case the Senate did not oppose the bill itself, but on a party vote of 38 to 17 it adopted an amendment permitting an appeal to the tariff board from the minister's decisions. It took this stand in the face of strong warnings from Diefenbaker that to do so would invoke punishment. Since the implication was that he would go to the country on the issue of Senate obstruction, and since it came at a time when the Liberals still felt quite unprepared for an election, Pearson's course involved genuine political brinkmanship. But it paid off.

The two parliamentary skirmishes represented more internal political fighting than Ottawa had seen in five years. The briskness of action stirred partisan passions on both sides. When Parliament quit for the summer, shortly after the two incidents, the general expectation was that Diefenbaker would get a dissolution and call a fall election. The Conservatives, although they knew they could not hope to repeat their record-breaking 1958 performance of winning 208 seats, were ready to fight. Most estimates at the time were that they could expect to return with 170 to 180 seats—a most comfortable majority—and settle down to another five years of power. Moreover, the Tory caucus reasoned that the longer an election was delayed, the more danger there was of losing seats.

But Diefenbaker delayed. As a man given to wavering in his decisions and not confiding his thinking to others or seeking their counsel, his reasons remain obscure. One element —among others—in his mind was a belief that if he waited long enough to permit the New Democratic Party to take hold under its new leader, Tommy Douglas, the effect would be to cut into Liberal strength and fragment the opposition. For the more radical elements of Canadian politics had chosen the summer of 1961 to merge the old socialistic Commonwealth Co-operative Federation with organized labor in an attempt to create an alternative opposition party under the New Democratic label.

But the merger of the agrarian CCF and the industrial forces of organized labor proved just as artificial in Canada as in splinter-party attempts in the United States. Douglas, a former minister and practiced swayer of political crowds, proved to have lost his forensic magic—or perhaps time had outdated his socialistic clichés.

By April, 1962, when Diefenbaker finally called the election for June, 1962, the power of timing it to his own advantage, which is one of the chief political weapons in a prime minister's hands, had all but passed from his grasp. Between fall and spring, Tory fortunes had indeed slumped still further. In the June balloting his massive majority shrank to a minority of 118. The Liberals doubled their membership to 100. The development that saved the Conservative government was not the farmer-labor forces of NDP but a revolt in Quebec against both the major parties, expressed in the election of twenty-six members running under the label of Social Credit, a party that had once been represented in Ottawa and controlled two western provinces but had become temporarily extinct nationally after 1958. A flashy eastern leader, Réal Caouette, had rallied his fellow French Canadians who were discontented with their lot in the Canadian national partnership into a protest vote based on the "what have you got to lose" principle. Like the *Poujade* movement in France, the *Créditistes* of Quebec puzzled the country and the politicians for a time. As a right-wing party, by rule of thumb they should have drawn off votes from the Conservatives; but instead they had prevented the Liberals from recapturing their historic Quebec majority, and enabled Diefenbaker to remain in office as a minority prime minister for an additional nine months.

13

The Summit

ON ELECTION night, June 18, 1962, Lester Pearson received the returns in an upstairs room at the red-brick headquarters of the National Liberal Federation at 251 Cooper Street in Ottawa. Around midnight he came down to the first-floor room where reporters and television cameras were awaiting his statement. The counting of ballots was still incomplete but it was clear that the Conservatives had been cut down below an absolute majority to 118 seats in the House of Commons and the Liberals lagged twenty members behind them, with forty-nine seats divided between the Social Credit and the New Democratic parties. For the fifth time in its history, Canada faced government by a minority.

Wearing a blue suit and sporting the bow tie that had been his early trade-mark in politics, Pearson took a seat at the table at which the TV cameras were aimed. As he awaited the cue informing him he was on the air, his eyes were focused

184

on some point outside the crowded room, his mind obviously harboring distant thoughts. But when the network switch to Liberal headquarters came through his words were crisp. Half a continent away, in Prince Albert, Saskatchewan, Diefenbaker had not yet said anything.

"It is clear," Pearson said, "that the Tory government has been decisively rejected. The government has suffered, after five years of rule with an unprecedented majority, a very decisive defeat."

He was, of course, accenting the positive. Within the hour Diefenbaker spoke from his home town to announce he would continue to serve as prime minister. It seemed to have been forgotten, the Prime Minister commented, that in 1921 Mackenzie King had received less than a majority but continued in office four years.

The thought bothering Pearson at the time of his statement, he revealed later, was that the inconclusive outcome meant he had to go through the ordeal again. "I realized at the end of that evening that we would be having to hold another election shortly, that would be the second act of the same play," he explained as he harked back to election night. "If we had been decisively beaten, then I would have retired, and the party would have been glad to have me retire, not on personal grounds, but because it would have been good for the party to have another leader.

"But we did well enough to make it very difficult to retire, though not well enough to win. Therefore there was no alternative but to go through it again. The prospect didn't cause me any great delight, but I thought, 'the sooner the better,' to get this over with."

There was considerable justification for the slant Pearson

put on the results. If the Liberals fell short of victory they had at least about doubled their strength. The Tories, however, had lost more than the Liberals gained, yielding seats to the splinter parties as well as to their prime foes. In the councils of the Liberal strategists in the weeks following the election, a firm decision was taken: to go all out in an attempt to overthrow the Diefenbaker government in the House and force an early election, exploiting the upswing psychology the party had achieved in the campaign.

It was a decision more easily made than implemented. Although Pearson loudly called for Parliament to reassemble at the earliest possible date, Diefenbaker cannily delayed the meeting until late September—to let political passions cool, as he explained. And after Parliament did convene, Liberal motions designed to upset the government were beaten down with regularity. Political campaigns are expensive, and none but the Liberals wanted another immediately; even among the Pearson ranks there were many back-benchers enjoying their first taste of Parliamentary status who had no desire to risk their fortunes soon again. Pearson could not muster the necessary support from the splinter groups. But the nearness of victory had imbued the Liberals with a spirit of aggression; all the other blocs were on the defensive.

Diefenbaker, particularly, suffered from shock over the results. During the campaign a foreign-exchange crisis had forced the government to devalue the Canadian dollar, and despite statistics supporting Tory claims that the economy itself was doing well, the Liberals charged Diefenbaker with having "deceived the people" in his claims about good business conditions. Actually the two parties were talking about two different things; but the Liberals had the better of the

186

argument when, immediately after the election, the exchange crisis worsened and the government was forced to borrow funds from abroad and impose tariff surcharges.

The charge of "deception" was almost more than Diefenbaker could bear. One July weekend at his country residence at Harrington Lake, near Ottawa, he stepped off a patio and broke a bone in his ankle. Lying in bed for several weeks while it healed, he brooded over his humiliation. Visitors who conferred with him reported him in a depressed state of mind, unable to make the numerous decisions facing him not only with respect to continuing the operation of the government but concerning the reorganization of the cabinet, which had lost five members by defeat. By early August, using crutches to get around the official residence, he had rallied sufficiently to fill the vacancies, shuffling some of the old members to new posts and promoting some parliamentary secretaries. He was particularly pleased over his success in recruiting a brand-new face in politics, M. Wallace McCutcheon, vice-president and general manager of Argus Corp., Ltd., a holding company with control over the vast industrial, merchandizing, and brewing interests of E. P. Taylor. Since McCutcheon was not a member of the House he was appointed Senator and made minister without portfolio, with duties undefined but in the general field of economic advice.

The strong man of the reorganized cabinet was an experienced politician of great common sense, tall, rough-hewn George Nowlan of Nova Scotia. He was shifted from the Ministry of National Revenue, a relatively minor post, to the key Ministry of Finance, replacing Fleming. Although Nowlan and McCutcheon had been only casually acquainted previously, they hit it off from the start, contributing complementary talents to the government. In short order they attracted a nucleus of orthodox conservatives around them within the cabinet ranks that gave the government a firmness of tone it did not have before.

The Diefenbaker government, though it carried the conservative label, had always been a somewhat unnatural alliance of agrarian radicals and eastern conservatives. The agrarian Progressives, whom Diefenbaker epitomized, were noted for their largesse to the farmers and their emphasis on measures conceived primarily for the sake of attracting votes. The newly influential conservative core believed that policies needed to be based on hardheaded economic judgments—that it was sounder long-run politics for the party to turn from political expediency to an attack on some of the country's basic problems.

For a time the Nowlan-McCutcheon group made headway. One of their early successes, for example, was to reverse the previous cabinet's policy of opposing sale of Canadian-produced electric power abroad—an issue that arose in connection with the Columbia River development treaty with the United States. Their argument was that Canada's biggest problem was reducing its outsize deficit in trade with the United States, which had been running at the rate of about $1 billion annually. Export of power was one item promising to make an important dent in the deficit. Another feature of the new conservative influence was a changed Canadian attitude toward Britain's entry into the European Common Market. During the period of London's active drive to join, before the French veto stymied British efforts, Canada gave the impression of obstruction. This obstruction was based on Canada's unwillingness to lose her preferential position as a commonwealth trading partner without having any constructive proposal of her own to offer. McCutcheon was particularly influential in persuading the cabinet that it behooved the country to be realistic and adapt itself to changes in trading patterns if Britain gained admittance to the European market. Nowlan added strength to the government because as a member of the House he had not made the personal enemies, nor harbored the petty grudges, that characterized Diefenbaker.

As the minority-run twenty-fourth Parliament wore on, the political antagonisms seemed to have settled into an uneasy deadlock that conceivably could last for the normal five years allotted to a government. Three factors broke the stalemate. Two were initiated by Mike Pearson; and one was a spectacular display by Diefenbaker of unwillingness to make a clear-cut decision on nuclear arms, which resulted in an unsuccessful cabinet revolt aimed at ousting Diefenbaker in favor of Nowlan. Failure of the plot led to the resignation of three ministers, and party morale sank to such low estate that three other ministers, for varying reasons, decided not to seek re-election.

The first Pearson initiative represented an attempt to produce action toward meeting the rising complaints of French Canada that she was not being given her equal share in the Canadian partnership. Just what it was that French Canada wanted had always been something of a mystery to English Canada; and as the English element, over the years, felt obliged to appease the French, the concessions were never more than superficial. For example, under Diefenbaker simultaneous translation was introduced in the House of Commons, giving French-speaking members the facility of being able to speak and listen in their own language as readily as the English could follow proceedings in theirs.

Pearson, though he did not have a solution for the French complaints, took the House floor on December 17, 1962, with a speech on the subject that impressed French-Canadian members with its recognition that the problem ran deep and needed searching exploration by men of intelligence and good will on both sides.

With Canada rapidly approaching the centenary of confederation, he said, it seemed strange that the nation was "doubtful and confused about our place and our role in a rapidly changing world." There was worry because Canada seemed more and more dependent on the United States economically, culturally, and even politically. Referring to the growing manifestations of provincial nationalism in Quebec, the movement toward "separatism" or secession, and the emergence of an undercover group styling itself the *Fédération Libération de Québec,* whose terrorist activities were reminiscent of what had been happening in Algeria, he said: "Recent events have shown clearly that we are going through another serious crisis of national unity, and I do not think it is an exaggeration to call it this. Not only have we been unable in this country to agree on all the symbols of nationhood long after we have become a nation, but in some quarters the very foundation of our confederation is being questioned."

Confederation, he went on, was Canada's declaration of faith in its own destiny, its declaration of independence from the United States. "We would go it on our own on this continent from coast to coast, first as part of the British Empire and later as an independent nation of the Commonwealth

190

of Nations. We knew at that time that such a declaration, based on such a faith, would involve an economic price. We were ready then in Canada to pay that price—and I hope and believe we are still ready to do so—namely, the price of being Canadian. Confederation, however, also involved another price which too many of us either forget or do not wish to pay because perhaps it is inconvenient for us to pay it. Confederation meant the rejection not only of political and economic annexation by the United States, but also of the American melting-pot concept of national unity. Confederation may not have been technically a treaty or a compact between states, but it was an understanding or a settlement between the two founding races of Canada made on the basis of an acceptable and equal partnership. That settlement provided that national political unity would be achieved and maintained without the imposition of racial, cultural, or linguistic uniformity."

As a result of the way in which Canada grew from coast to coast, and Quebec remained in insular isolation under a system of education that did not fit its people for competition in industrial development going on in the rest of the country, he said, it was understandable that two different interpretations would grow up.

"To French-speaking Canadians," Pearson said, "confederation created a bilingual and bicultural nation. It protected their language and their culture throughout the whole of Canada. It meant partnership, not domination. French-speaking Canadians believed that this partnership meant equal opportunities for both founding races to share in all phases of Canadian development. English-speaking Canadians agree, of course, that the confederation arrangements protected the rights of French Canadians in Quebec, in Parliament, and in federal courts; but most felt—and I think it is fair to say this —that it did not go beyond those limits, at least until recently. This meant that for all practical purposes, there would be an English-speaking Canada with a bilingual Quebec. What is called the 'French Fact' was to be provincial only."

Pearson credited the English element with no lack of good will and with an awareness that "something was happening in Quebec" as the province emerged from its insularity after the end of World War II. "But perhaps we needed shock treatment to make us appreciate the full significance of what had happened, of Quebec's social revolution. That shock was given in recent years by separatism, by the agitation in some quarters, which got so much publicity, for what was called political liberation. That was an extreme reaction to what had been going on for at least 15 years in industrial and social change."

The answer to the problem, he contended, depended in part on French-speaking Canadians themselves, on their willingness to continue the effort begun in 1960 to develop the educational facilities designed to qualify their people to exploit the opportunities and fulfill the responsibilities of modern life. But the answer also depended, "and I believe in greater degree, on English-speaking Canadians, because we are in the majority."

His proposal for action, put into effect after he became prime minister, was the appointment of a royal commission comprising distinguished Canadians of both races, to undertake a searching examination of the facts and make recommendations for solution. Pearson's speech evoked important response in French Canada. Politically it offered a Quebec that had become thoroughly disillusioned with the Tories on this issue, the chance to support something more positive than mere protest, which the election of Social Credit members had, to a large degree, represented.

But in political terms, Pearson's second initiative canceled out any advantage he might have reaped in Quebec. In a speech to Toronto's York-Scarborough Liberal Association on January 12, 1963, he came out for Canadian acquisition of nuclear warheads. Quebec, more than any other part of Canada, was opposed to nuclear weapons. In both world wars French Canada's attitude had been antimilitarist, pacifist, even neutralist, and opposition to nuclear arms was in keeping with the tradition.

Pearson took his nuclear stand in awareness of its effect in Quebec, and also in the knowledge that he would be accused of inconsistency, for it represented a sharp reversal of previous attitudes. At the 1961 Liberal rally the party had adopted a resolution advocating that Canada withdraw from active combat participation in the U.S.-Canadian North American Air Defense Command and confine itself to "detection, identification, and warning"—a role derided by some in Canada as "bird watching." This caused the New York *Daily News* to suggest editorially that a royal commission, including psychiatrists, be appointed to find out "what ails Pearson." In the House of Commons, on August 4, 1960, the Liberal party position was set forth officially, with Pearson's approval, by the party's "defense critic," Paul Hellyer. It consisted of eleven points, including: "Canada should immediately end the NORAD agreement"; air defense being impossible in the thermonuclear age, "Canada should quit building Bomarc sites and should not replace the CF-100" interceptor with which the Royal Canadian Air Force was equipped; "no nuclear weapons should be permitted on or over Canadian soil"; Canada must "urge on NATO a fundamental revision of its present nuclear strategy coupled with a reorganization of its forces so that any aggression with conventional weapons can be repulsed with conventional weapons."

Pearson reversed all this with his Toronto speech. In Canada it is the party leader's prerogative to set policy regardless of party resolutions. Having decided that the old policy was obsolete, he said:

"Today, defense policy is based more on the interdependence, than the independence, of nations. No country, not even the most powerful, can defend itself alone. The only security, especially for a country like Canada, lies in collective action through a defensive alliance such as NATO, which rests, or should rest, insofar as its military side is concerned, on a pooling of strength. Collective defense of this kind is based on treaties; on obligations undertaken, and on commitments given . . .

"To find the best defense policy for Canada would be a difficult enough problem in any circumstance and for any government. But it has been complicated and confused by the controversy over one aspect of policy; whether to use nuclear weapons of any kind, or not to use them. Whether Canada, in present circumstances, uses nuclear weapons or not, cannot, however, be decided on moral grounds without hypocrisy on our part. As a member of the NATO coalition we accept the nuclear deterrent in the hands of the United States as essential for defense, and we supply much of the uranium that goes into American nuclear bombs."

What, then, should Canada do? "It should end at once its

evasion of responsibility, by discharging the commitments it has already accepted for Canada. It can only do this by accepting nuclear warheads for those defensive tactical weapons which cannot effectively be used without them but which we have agreed to use. An agreement with the United States for this purpose would have to be negotiated ... Action taken under such an agreement would ensure that the air division in NATO or the Bomarc squadrons for continental defense would have these weapons available, would be trained in their use, and would be ready in an emergency to do the job entrusted to them by the Canadian government after agreement with our allies."

Two factors changed Pearson's mind. One was the Cuban crisis of October, 1962, when President Kennedy, in the greatest display of "brinkmanship" to date, ordered Khrushchev to take his missiles out of Cuba or face attack on Soviet Russia. "It was the Cuban thing, more than anything else, that changed my mind," Pearson said later in explaining his motives for the policy switch. "It was the thought that here we were, a part of continental defense, on the eve of this possible great tragedy, and we were completely impotent, as far as Canada was concerned, impotent." The impact of Cuba was difficult to take. "Sentimentally I felt I was operating against my instincts in the past, which were that we should not have anything to do with these things."

There was, however, an additional factor. In November Paul Hellyer, later to become Pearson's defense minister, made a trip to Europe as member of a parliamentary delegation visiting NATO bases. He had not seen the bases since 1955. His report to Pearson after his return confirmed the judgment Pearson already was beginning to make; it represented as much of a switch for Hellyer as for Pearson.

"I was struck by two things," says Hellyer. "The morale of Canadian forces and other Canadians in Europe was in sharp contrast to 1955. They were frustrated, despondent, bewildered. The other thing was the attitude of our allies. Our reputation as a nation that could be counted on to perform its commitments and carry through on them was beginning to suffer. It was being talked about informally in NATO circles and it obviously was soon going to reach the NATO council as a subject for formally recognized discussion."

The reason for this state of affairs was that while both Diefenbaker and his defense minister, Douglas Harkness, had often said that Canada's defense forces were entitled to the best modern weapons available, the decision to acquire war heads for the four types of nuclear weapons possessed by Canada had been postponed so long that it had become an open scandal. At home two Bomarc missile bases had been installed, and supersonic Voodoo interceptors acquired from the United States to replace obsolete *CF-100*'s. In Europe Canadian artillery units had their Honest John batteries but the warheads were filled with sand; the Canadian air squadrons were receiving their first Starfighter strike-reconnaissance planes, the last of the weapons to come into use, but they lacked their nuclear armament. November 1 had been a final deadline to make arrangements for acquiring nuclear warheads—if the Canadian NATO elements were to be ready to fulfill their role and cover their assigned targets in the overall plan for NATO readiness, by the time the last of the Starfighters were delivered in April, 1963.

But in Ottawa the government still stalled. Defense Minister Harkness, who favored nuclear weapons, had believed periodically for about two years that he had the cabinet on the verge of agreement to undertake the arrangements to acquire warheads, but always there was some reason for postponement. He was a sadly frustrated man by January, 1963, when General Lauris Norstad, making the round of NATO capitals in connection with his retirement as NATO commander, put the Canadian government on the spot. At a press conference in Ottawa, Norstad said Canada had accepted a commitment its NATO forces were not equipped to fulfill.

When Parliament, soon afterward, debated defense policy, Diefenbaker categorically denied that Canada had repudiated any international commitment. Any such statement, he said, was "false in substance and false in fact." Ever since Cuba, Diefenbaker insisted, Canada had been "forcibly" negotiating with the U.S. "so that nuclear warheads would be readily available in case of need." His statement brought a rather dryly worded reply from the State Department that while discussions of an "exploratory" nature had been instituted, "The Canadian government has not as yet proposed any arrangement sufficiently practical to contribute effectively to North American defense."

Harkness, who wanted to make a clear-cut statement on defense policy and saw Diefenbaker once again clothe the issue with ambiguous statements, resigned in disgust. But Harkness was not the only member fed up with Diefenbaker's eternal ambiguity and delay. On the night of February 5 all three opposition parties united against the government, voting no confidence twice, by identical tallies of 142 to 111. Diefenbaker announced he would call on the governor general next day to advise dissolution of Parliament. This led to the election of April 8.

In the weeks that followed the government's downfall the Liberals put on a flashy, well-merchandised campaign featuring a promise of "Sixty Days of Decision" after taking office. It was a dazzling promise to a country heartily sick of equivocating, although it produced some hasty and ill-considered action when put into effect after the Liberals won power. Basically, however, it had been Pearson's two initiatives that had sparked movement in a stalemated political situation. Basically it was Diefenbaker's insistence on straddling the nuclear issue that compassed his repudiation by the voters. Even in the Liberal camp there were those who, in hindsight, felt Diefenbaker had contributed more to Pearson's election than Pearson himself.

And so, on Monday, April 22, 1963, Lester Bowles Pearson put on his striped pants and black morning coat and went to pay a call on the governor general of Canada, Major General George P. Vanier, in order to be sworn in as the queen's first minister in Canada. The courtly old officer, who had been Vincent Massey's number-two man at Canada House in London when Pearson got his first foreign post as number-three man, performed the ceremony in a second-floor bedroom of his residence, Rideau Hall, since he was still recovering from a light heart attack. Then the new prime minister presented the twenty-four men and one woman whom he had picked to form his cabinet. Five of them had served in previous Liberal cabinets and, with a few others who had survived the lean Liberal years, they gave the group its weighting of experience in politics. The others were mostly young men who had been attracted to politics by the example of Pearson himself. With this balance of veterans and vigor, the man who had been drawn somewhat reluctantly into each stage of political contest prepared to undertake the fateful task of governing Canada.

14

To Put Meaning in Unity

CANADIANS, if they only knew it, do have an
identity separate from that of the United States. True, in a
national sense, it is an English identity, with Yankee tinges.
But it is a distinct identity nevertheless, and an attractive one.

One symbol of it is the U-shaped quadrangle of buildings
on Parliament Hill in Ottawa: the houses of parliament dom-
inated by the Peace Tower, backed by the Parliamentary Library and flanked by the East Block and West Block, topping
a magnificent bluff overlooking the Ottawa River near where
the early *voyageurs* portaged in their canoe-bearing penetra-
tions of the continental interior. The sense of historical con-
tinuity hangs heavier in Canada than in the U.S.; 1867 is by
no means as much of a cut-off date as 1776. As is only fitting,
the parliament building itself vaguely recalls that of the
mother legislature in London, though its architecture has
been described as "Presbyterian Gothic." Silhouetted against

a western sunset, the buildings on "the Hill" are somehow suggestive of a Canadian Kremlin, though their nineteenth-century spires are topped with what looked like cowbells to the first prime minister, Sir John A. Macdonald, instead of with onions. It is on the greensward within the quadrangle that each morning during the summer tourist season the red-coated, bearskin-hatted, foot-stamping soldiers change guard as if performing at Buckingham Palace. From the Peace Tower, at stated intervals during the week as well as on special occasions, the carillon peals out melody over the center of town in one of the pleasanter aspects of small-capital living.

Ritualistically Canada still preserves the forms of Westminster; and to an American long removed from his ancestral renunciation of the trappings of monarchy, the rituals convey a nostalgic charm. In Washington, when the House of Representatives meets each day, a minor functionary casually ambles into the chamber with the mace and deposits it in its pedestal. In Ottawa each day's session involves a little ceremony that never palls. The speaker, wearing the black robe, white collar, and tricorn black hat of his office, marches from his chambers through the rotunda to the House floor, preceded by the black-robed clerks and the sword-toting sergeant-at-arms bearing the gilded mace over his shoulder, the mace to be deposited reverently in the brackets before the dais.

The formal opening of a Canadian parliament is only a shade less colorful than that of London. If the weather permits, the governor general and his lady ride in an open coach from Rideau Hall, preceded by Mounties with pennants on their lances, to review the guard of honor and then, in the red-carpeted Senate chamber, the governor general reads the

Speech from the Throne. For this occasion the Senate's Gentleman Usher of the Black Rod is sent across the building to summon the members of the House. Black Rod's knock on the closed doors of the House never fails to bring a hush; his slow progress up the length of the green-carpeted chamber, punctuated by three pauses to bow to the speaker, receives rapt attention.

The cadences of a tongue used by the court of Elizabeth I in the days when Sir Francis Drake was making his voyages to the new world still ring in the halls when new senators are "summoned" to sit in the upper chamber and receive their sovereign's instruction: "We do command you, that all difficulties and excuses whatsoever laying aside, you be and appear for the purposes aforesaid, in the Senate of Canada at all times and wheresoever our Parliament may be in Canada convoked and holden; and this you are in no wise to omit." What American can fail to be stirred by a nostalgic kinship with traditions that extend all the way back to Runnymede? Or who would scoff at the harmless pretense, when a session's supply bills are voted, that the appropriations bill containing all the funds theoretically grants some $6 billion or more to her gracious majesty, Queen Elizabeth II, with which to operate her government in Canada for another twelvemonth? Ritual at least does not extend to asking the queen to sign all the checks.

The forms are British; the people so like Americans—most of them—as to be practically indistinguishable. No wonder that French Canada feels left out in the cold.

What is it the French Canadian wants? For as long as English Canadians have been aware of dissatisfaction among their French Canadian partners, so long has this puzzled them. In general the attitude of the English Canadian would seem to be like that of Professor Henry Higgins, unable to understand why Eliza Doolittle would act in such an exasperating, irrational, irritating way as to want to leave his household. Higgins is obviously an intelligent man, yet he asks: "Pickering, why can't a woman be more like a man?" Thus the average, intelligent English-speaking Canadian asks himself a similar question about his French-speaking compatriot, unconsciously paraphrasing Higgins: "We are so honest, so thoroughly square, eternally noble, historically fair; who, when you win, will always give your back a pat." Why can't the French Canadians be like that?

An outsider can only conclude that what the French Canadian wants is nothing more than to be loved. His desire for equality of respect and equal treatment in the partnership is akin to Eliza Doolittle's yearning to be recognized as something more than an instrument through which Henry Higgins can display his linguistic talents.

The political marriage of French and English Canada was not a love match, being based on prior armed conquest of the French by the English. The French bride knew that one motivation of the English groom was a desire to avoid being forced into a marriage with a siren to the south, and she exacted contract terms designed to insure that the marriage would be more than one of convenience. But as the groom went about his business in the world at large and the bride in effect stayed at home, it was inevitable that they would drift apart mentally and emotionally, leading to periodic scenes of recrimination on the bride's part and annoyed frustration on the groom's.

This family quarrel now has become most acute. The

genius of Mackenzie King, who was prime minister for nearly twenty-two years of this century, was his ability to keep the clash from breaking up the family. Incredibly petty and self-seeking as King may have been, he did preserve Canadian unity, after a fashion, at least sufficiently to see the nation through the crisis of the greatest war.

But in the upheavals this century has seen, and particularly in the enormous political ferment that has taken place since World War II, merely "preserving unity" is not enough. The backward countries are the ones that have fragmented, breaking up colonial territories into small nation units based more on tribal pride and jealousies than on viable economies. Africa has provided the sharpest demonstration of this trend among the politically immature. The mature, adult nations, have at the same time shown a strong tendency toward closer federation and interdependence.

Canada, as a politically mature nation in all but one respect, has reached a stage in history when it must resolve this internal conflict if it is to achieve its rightful status among the nations of the democratic world.

Lester B. Pearson intends, if he can, to make Canada's unity meaningful. As a diplomat he displayed a distinct flair for taking political risks to achieve results. The measure of his stature as a prime minister will be his ability to apply the same skill toward persuading his countrymen that there is a national-character potential in Canada that is greater than the sum of its two chief cultures.

Index

Gouin, Sir Lomer, 42
Graves, Robert, 30
Green, Howard, 118
Greer, Harold, 166–67
Grierson, John, 48
"Grits," 22n
Grossart, Allister, 151–53
Guelph Maple Leafs, 24

Halifax, Lord, 84
Hamilton, Ont., 25, 33
Hamilton Collegiate, 26
Hammarskjold, Dag, 100, 111, 113, 117
Harkness, Douglas, 196, 197
Harris, Walter, 102, 132–33, 138
Harvey, Oliver, 79
Hatch, Carl, 82
Hees, George, 147
Hellyer, Paul, 193, 195–96
Hickerson, John, 81
Holmes, John, 123
Hopkins, Harry, 75–76
Howe, C. D., 75, 89, 133, 163, 178
Hughes, Gen. Sam, 28
Hull, Cordell, 78

Ignatiev, George, 123, 126, 128
Independent Social Credit Party, 4n
Ismay, Gen. H. L., 81

Jebb, Gladwyn, 100
Johnson, Harry G., 164–65

Kaganovich, Lazar, 126
Keenlyside, Hugh, 39
Kent, Tom, 135–36, 153, 155–56, 166, 169, 175–76
Khrushchev, Nikita, 123, 126–29
King, William Lyon Mackenzie, 42, 46, 50, 52, 60, 63, 64, 66–67, 71, 73, 75, 76, 81, 83–84, 85, 87, 133, 204
Kirkwood, Kenneth P., 39
Korean crisis in the United Nations, 106–8
Kutusof, Marshal, 129

La Guardia, Fiorello, 83, 85
LaMontagne, Maurice, 153, 166, 176
Lascelles, Thomas, 64
Laurier, Sir Wilfred, 6, 54, 133
League of Nations, 42, 49–50
Lehman, Herbert, 83
Liberal Party
  elections
    1957, 131–35
    1958, 149–50
    1962, 182–87
    1963, 4, 4n, 134, 198–99
  "Grits," 22n
  1961 rally and resolutions
  Pearson as Leader and Leader of Opposition (1958–63), 3, 136–98
  plans for and platform of reorganization at Kingston conference, 159–66
Lie, Trygve, 98, 99
Lodge, Henry Cabot, 100, 112, 115
London, 48–69
Low, Solon, 149

McCarthy, Leighton, 73, 74
McCutcheon, M. Wallace, 187–88
Macdonald, Mary, 176
Macdonald, Sir John, 23, 25
MacDonald, Ross, 180
MacEachen, Allan J., 176
McGarvin, Mike, 26
Mackenzie, Alexander, 23
Mackenzie, Michael, 154
Macville, Ont., 21
Malenkov, Georgi, 124
Malinovsky, Marshal, 162
Martin, Paul, 98, 122–23, 132–33, 140–42
Massey, Vincent, 9, 26–27, 42, 43, 48, 63, 69, 75
Massey, Mrs. Vincent, 62
Meighen, Arthur, 42
Menon, Krishna, 119
Merchant, Livingston, 11–12
Molotov, V. M., 121–25
Mono Road, Ont., 21
Montreal Financial Times, 162
Mowat, Oliver, 23